Coaching, Mentoring and Managing

Edited by
Dr. William Hendricks
with
Sam Bartlett, Joe Gilliam, Kit Grant,
Jack Mackey, Bob Norton, Jim Siress,
Jim Stanley and Randall Wright

CAREER PRESS
3 Tice Road
P.O. Box 687
Franklin Lakes, NJ 07417
1-800-CAREER-1
201-848-0310 (NJ and outside U.S.)
FAX: 201-848-1727

COACHING, MENTORING AND MANAGING
ISBN 1-56414-243-4, $16.99
Cover design by The Visual Group
Cover photo by Tony Stone Images
Printed in the U.S.A. by Book-mart Press

To order this title by mail, please include price as noted above, $2.50 handling per
order, and $1.00 for each book ordered. Send to: Career Press, Inc., 3 Tice Road.,
P.O. Box 687, Franklin Lakes, NJ 07417.

Or call toll-free 1-800-CAREER-1 (NJ and Canada: 201-848-0310) to order using
VISA or MasterCard, or for further information on books from Career Press.

Library of Congress Cataloging-in-Publication Data

Coaching, mentoring and managing / edited by William Hendricks ...
 [et al.].
   p.   cm.
 Includes index.
 ISBN 1-56414-243-4 (pbk.)
   1. Mentoring in business. 2. Employees—Training of.
 3. Employees—Counseling of.   I. Hendricks, William, Dr.
 HF5385.C63 1996
 658.3'124—dc2O   95-50919
                                                                      CIP

Legend Symbol Guide

Key issues to learn and understand for future application.

Questions that will help you apply the critical points to your situation.

Interactive exercises that reinforce your learning experience.

Checklist that will help you identify important issues for future application.

C
A
S
E

S
T
U
D
Y
Real-world case studies that will help you apply the information you've learned.

Legend Symbol Guide (continued)

CASE STUDY ANALYSIS

Analysis of case study, with applications and practical use.

CASE SUMMARY

EXERCISE

Exercise that will stimulate thought and creativity.

$\mathcal{P}$REFACE

"Oh, this is just great," you may be saying as you give the once-over to the title of this book, *Coaching, Mentoring and Managing*. "With everything else I've got to do as a manager, now I'm expected to become a *coach*, too!?!"

Well, there's good news and bad news. Grim realities first: If you manage people, you're *already* a coach. Don't believe it? Then ask yourself, "Who is expected to motivate, inspire, instruct, lead and correct the people who work for me?" You know the answer to that one — it's *you*, coach! Will you reap the enormous benefits your role as coach can bring to you and your company? Or will you sit on the sidelines while your people fumble again and again? The choice is yours.

So what's the good news, you ask? The good news — actually, the *great* news! — is that this practical Business User's Manual reveals how highly successful and innovative managers have tapped into an unlimited resource — their own people — by learning the secrets of StaffCoaching™. Imagine being able to learn from the nation's leading experts on coaching and counseling. Imagine that you could gather more than 200 years of success into a real plan of action.

You'll get step-by-step, point-by-point example after interesting example, and you'll discover how these winning strategies can work for you.

The tips on how to ask open-ended questions, for instance, (see Chapter 5) are alone worth the price of this book. Never again will you be reduced to fuming at a well-meaning employee, "What in the world made you *do* such a dumb thing?" (There's a better way — we promise!)

Let's face it. Regardless of how you as a manager feel about coaching, your people want to play on a winning team. Everyone does. Read and absorb the practical information on StaffCoaching™ in this book, then inspire your team to go the distance!

CONTENTS

Chapter 1 New Productivity that Starts with You ... 1

Understanding the Manager's Role as Coach 1
The 10 Values of a Successful StaffCoach™ 2
What You Value Will Impact Your Team 19
Now What? 22
Five Insights of High-Performance Coaches 23
Chapter Quiz 31

Chapter 2 The Five-Step StaffCoaching™ Model 33

A Performance Process that Starts Right
Where You Are 33
Knowing Your Employees' Character and
Capabilities: Four Effective Approaches 36
Now What? 45
What's Your StaffCoaching™ Style? An Inventory
that Tells You 46
So What? 48
Six Pitfalls to Your StaffCoaching™ Success 48
What Do You Think? 54
10 Tools for Building a Solid Team Foundation 55
Chapter Quiz 70

Chapter 3 The Coaching Role.............................71

What Is the Coaching Role?.................................72
The Coach's Role in Communicating Involvement
and Establishing Trust..74
The Coach's Role in Clarifying Expectations and
Verifying Understanding.....................................81
The Coach's Role in Affirming the Team.........................94
The Coach's Role in Motivating and Inspiring................98
Eight Hurdles to Performing Your Coaching Role 102
What to Expect When You're Doing It Right 116
Chapter Quiz...125

Chapter 4 The Mentoring Role:
Instruction by Example 127

Making Great Strides by "Walking Alongside" 127
A Process with Productive Purpose 128
The Six Ways People Think...133
The Three Key Phases of Successful Mentoring............141
The Outcome of Effective Mentoring..............................149
The Treasure of Mentoring 155
Chapter Quiz 156

Chapter 5 The Counseling Role:
Confrontation and Correction........................157

Four Keys to Effective Counseling 157
The Philosophy of Confrontation: a Positive Approach
to Negative Events...161
The Five-Step Confrontation Process 164
Eight Ways to Eliminate Unsatisfactory Behavior..........168
10 Freeing Essentials of Face-to-Face Counseling.........176
Five Steps to Modifying Behavior..................................183
How to Ask Questions that Get the Answers
You Need...187
Recognizing the Results of Counseling that Works.......189
Chapter Quiz 193

Chapter 6 The High-Performance Team **195**
    Instilling Team Vision 195
    Recognizing the Potential for Team Trouble 198
    A Checklist for Responding to Team Troubles 205
    "Look Before You Leap" Checklist 209
    The Freeing Power of Team Priorities 210
    Right Thinking About Team Purpose 214
    Chapter Quiz 215

Chapter 7 Stay in Control of Your
    StaffCoaching™ Role **217**
    Choosing Your StaffCoaching™ Role Based on
    Personality 220
    Four Points on Which StaffCoaching™ Stands or Falls .225
    Five Ways to Quiet Complaints 226
    Applying the Four "P's" 228
    Chapter Quiz 230

Chapter 8 Conclusion **231**
    "StaffCoach™ Values" Scenarios 232

Index **243**

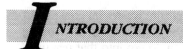INTRODUCTION

Across the nation, managers are finding out that management skills must change. To get the most from the workforce and compete successfully in international markets, today's manager must be more than a boss — he or she must be a coach.

This management-changing resource was designed by today's most renowned experts in coaching and counseling. These professionals will lead you to new levels of effectiveness and challenge you to make a difference in the lives of those you work with. Each chapter is filled with real-world advice and management-changing exercises these professionals have used and developed for organizations and managers like you.

As a manager, isn't your role much like that of a coach? Your team members all have different talents and skill levels — they're all human with strengths, shortcomings and personal lives that sometimes affect their ability to perform at work. And regardless of how difficult it may be at times, you are responsible for "winning" with that special mix of people ... for keeping your people inspired, motivated and working together toward team goals.

The greatest coaches are those who know how to motivate others to succeed, stay focused, believe in themselves and overcome disappointments. Coaches inspire others to aim higher, work harder ... and enjoy doing it!

Research proves that business typically wastes its greatest resource: the people who work for it. **Coaching, Mentoring and Managing** will teach you how to tap into that resource. You will learn how to motivate and inspire your work team. You will learn how to build trust and commitment with your staff. You will learn how to identify your personal strengths and weaknesses as a StaffCoach™, plus how to focus the energy of your team and get the most out of the people who work for you.

UNLIMITED POSSIBILITIES

What do managers and coaches get paid to do? To produce results — to win. And they do that through one or more of three resources: time, money and people.

Let's take a closer look at these three resources. Time is a limited resource, right? Money is also a limited resource (for some of us, it's a *very* limited resource!). But what about people? It may come as a surprise, but research shows that the people who work for us can be *unlimited* resources. Now, you may be thinking, "Ha! You don't know who works for *me!*" But this manual is expressly designed to (1) prove that any employee can be an unlimited resource and (2) teach you how to tap into that resource.

Henry Kissinger once said, "Leaders take their people from where they are to where they've never been before." That's what your role as coach will help you do — take your staff members from where they are (limited) to where they've never been before (unlimited).

INVESTING IN THE RIGHT RESOURCES

As a manager and coach, you should remember three critical facts:

1. *Management means getting things done through others.* Your job as a leader is to work through the people who work for you. That's how you'll get results from your team.

    Ferdinand Fournies, who wrote *Coaching for Improved Work Performance,* said, "When you do everything yourself, you're just a technician. When you get things done through others, that's when you become a leader."

If you are doing any part of your job because "No one else is doing it, so I have to" or because "No one does it as well as I do, so I do it," you're probably not getting the best results you could. You're spending time on things other people ought to do.

2. *You need your people more than they need you.* Why? Because the only way you're going to get results is through them. You can't do every job. Your time is a limited resource. Only your team can get everything done.

3. *You get paid for what your people do ... not for what you do.* This is crucial to understand. If it's true that the people who work for you are helping you get results, then what they're doing, you get paid for!

In light of these three facts, you can begin to make some decisions about where you should invest your time and energies as a leader: in your people ... in your team. No other investment will pay higher dividends than an investment in your people.

IT ALL COMES DOWN TO WINNING

Managers who assume the role of coach immediately begin to invest their time and energy in their people. This focus to produce a winning performance is called StaffCoaching™. Based on the principles winning coaches use to inspire their teams to excel, ***Coaching, Mentoring and Managing*** will help you make the most of each employee's special talents and harness your group's combined energy to create a results-focused team. The confidence you have in your own abilities — and the respect you gain from your staff and management alike — will increase as you use the principles in this manual to create an environment where employees enjoy their work, exude positive attitudes, "buy in" to company policies and team goals and willingly take on added responsibilities.

Whether your team numbers 3 or 300, the principles you are about to learn can deliver winning results for you!

C HAPTER 1

New Productivity that Starts with You

"All the coaching in the world will fall short if the behavior you expect is not honored and recognized."
— Sam Bartlett

UNDERSTANDING COACHING, MENTORING AND MANAGING

You might think the ability to be a good coach is something you have to be born with. Actually, everyone can develop the skills, the personal techniques — the attitude — to successfully coach other people. You can learn how to improve your coaching skills and become a person who inspires others to give 110 percent!

First, though, you must *want* to be a coach. What is your attitude about being a coach as you are reading this? Is it positive? Do you truly understand the need to be an effective coach? Do you grasp how important it is to be a *good* coach? These facts shape your attitude about being a coach, *because people act on what they believe or "value."* The most enlightening facts about great leadership are worthless until someone decides to use them ... to actually apply these truths

> *Everyone can develop the skills, the personal techniques — the attitude — to successfully coach other people.*

Sam Bartlett is a consultant, conference speaker and author. He has provided consulting and on-site training for Caterpillar, TVA, and Southern Methodist University, along with many other organizations. He currently trains close to a thousand business leaders each month through public seminars. Participants from Fortune 500 companies consistently rank his workshops as "the best they have ever attended." Sam lives in Maitland, Florida, where he is the president of Alliance Performance Institute.

> *"First say to yourself what you would be; then do what you have to do."*
>
> *— Epictetus*

in the job setting. And that happens only when managers believe there is potential "value" as a result of their actions.

So let's consider the values that successful StaffCoaches™ typically exhibit. Although you will have many additional values of your own, here are the 10 key values reported by leaders in work environments very much like yours.

THE 10 VALUES OF A SUCCESSFUL STAFFCOACH™

1. **Clarity** — A strong sense of direction and purpose.

2. **Supportiveness** — A commitment to stand with and behind team members.

3. **Confidence-building** — A personal commitment to build and sustain the self-image of each team member.

4. **Mutuality** — A true partnership orientation.

5. **Perspective** — An unflappable focus on the entire business enterprise.

6. **Risk** — The encouragement of effort that reduces punishment for mistakes and encourages learning in all things.

7. **Patience** — A view of time and performance that equitably balances learning and business demands.

8. **Involvement** — A genuine commitment to allow team members to control their work.

9. **Confidentiality** — An ability to protect the information of all team business.

10. **Respect** — A commitment to value and see the treasure within your people.

Successful coaches possess 10 key values, plus the character and personality traits that make them effective. You can and should incorporate these values into your personal leadership style.

1. Clarity

Successful StaffCoaches™ make sure they communicate clearly. If your communication isn't clear, what happens? People start to fail or do nothing — or worse, they make assumptions. And assumptions always cost time and money. If you want to make sure your communication is clear, NEVER assume your team members know what you want.

Example:

Printing department on phone:
Bev, we're ready to print this rush job of yours now, but I thought you said you wanted us to print it in three colors.

Bev/Manager:
I *do* want three colors.

Printer:
Well, we only got two sets of film from the film department. They say that's all you ordered. They gave us film for the red and the yellow.

Bev/Manager:
... and black. What about black?

Printer:
It's not here. Did you tell them to provide black film?

Bev/Manager:
Everyone in the film department saw the color layout. I assumed they knew I would be using black. I certainly wouldn't print photos of people in red or yellow.

Printer:
I don't think they assumed that. And if I have to wait for more film, I can't deliver when you said you needed it ...

An understandable oversight. It's easy to forget that black is a color to people who work with film. In this case, however, an understandable assumption caused everyone involved time and money. How can you be sure you're not assuming? Ask questions that reveal what people are thinking, such as:

Assumptions always cost time and money.

3

Is there anything I've said that might still be a little unclear?

How do you think this approach will work?

What kinds of problems do you think we should anticipate?

Is there anything you might add to this process that would improve it?

Tell me what you believe you and I have agreed you will do.

Clarity isn't found exclusively in how the coach communicates to his team members — it's listening and responding to their attempts to open revealing lines of communication.

Coach:
So you and Jim feel good about making this deadline, Ray?

Ray:
We've done it dozens of times.

Coach:
I just want to make sure I can promise the client we'll be there as agreed.

Ray:
Well, you can promise we'll do *our* part — I can't promise the equipment will hold up under that kind of volume. But we'll find a way. We always do.

Did you hear two messages in that dialogue? The first message was, "We'll do it." The second was, "We might *not* do it." It's tempting to assume that the first message will prevail, especially when schedules are tight and the client is important or impatient ... or both. But an attentive, realistic coach will look into *secondary* messages communicated by his people. If you don't, you risk more than deadline surprise. You risk having your people hear two messages from *you*: (1) don't bother me with particulars, just get it done, and (2) your problems aren't as important to me as how we look to the client.

> *"You only succeed when people are communicating, not just from the top down but in complete interchanges. Communication comes from fighting off my ego and listening."*
>
> **Bill Walsh**

In this case, the coach may have equipment problems that are about to create client headaches — and may have already created morale problems.

2. Supportiveness

Supportiveness means standing behind the people on your team ... providing the help they need, whether that help means advice, information, materials, or just understanding and encouragement. It's important to communicate your intention to be supportive.

Let your team members know early (individually or in a group setting) that they are part of a unit ... a team whose members pull together. Let them know that honest mistakes or problems aren't terminal. In fact, problems will only make the team stronger as you learn to solve them together. Most importantly, let them know that you are behind them all the way. You exist to help the team win by maximizing individual skills, not by forcing each member to do his job exactly as you or someone else might. You want each member to become the best he can be.

Sound radical? Twenty years ago, maybe. Not today. Supportiveness is a critical value to coaches who succeed nationwide, and it is refreshing, uplifting news to members of any team. Here's an example of how a coach can show responsible support:

Supervisor:
This design modification I tried didn't work, Terry. I was sure it would, but they tell me we've got to come up with a new design, and that will slow us down at least three days. I guess I blew it.

Coach:
Isn't this the job you worked on your own time to finish?

Supervisor:
Yes. A weekend.

> *Let your team know that honest mistakes or problems aren't terminal.*

Coach:

Well, naturally I wish the design had worked — but two of the three days it will cost us to redo it haven't really been *spent* yet, anyway. You donated them. What if we put two additional people on it? Could we cut a day off the delay time?

Supervisor:

We probably could.

Coach:

Let's try it. If we make it, we break even time-wise. And if we don't, well, you gave it your best shot. Next time, when the time is this tight, let's try brainstorming the design approach with four or five of the other designers before committing to an approach.

Supervisor:

Good idea. Thanks, Pat.

The opposite of supporting is controlling. If you aren't supporting, you are controlling. And the managers who control are the ones who don't get the best from their people. If you control the project or plan, people will feel mistrusted and stifled.

Ted (Customer Service Rep on phone):

Hello. This is Ted Stevens.

Customer (on phone):

Mr. Stevens, this is Phil from ACME. We have a problem with the shipment we received this morning from you.

Ted:

Let me get your records up on the computer, Phil. OK, I've got it. What's the problem?

Customer:

It's incomplete! I spoke with your department head yesterday afternoon and explained how we just had a rush order come in. He promised that he would put an extra 200 shafts on the truck this morning with our regular order.

> *If you aren't supporting, you are controlling.*

Ted:
Hmm. I don't see any record here of that. You say Mr. Ingles approved the extra parts to be shipped?

Customer:
That's right. And we need them TODAY!

Ted:
Well ... I really don't know what to do for you. My records don't show Mr. Ingles approving the add-on, and I can't ship more out without his signature.

Customer:
Then get Mr. Ingles on the phone for me. We need those parts NOW!

Ted:
Well, uh, Mr. Ingles isn't here right now.

Customer:
Then *you* take care of it! After all, we've been customers with you for more than 10 years!

Ted:
I'm sorry, but Mr. Ingles has a strict policy that special orders MUST have his approval, and he won't be in until ...

Customer:
Well, you tell Mr. Ingles for me that we won't be bothering you again with orders when they are important to us!

Ted didn't provide very good customer service. He probably knows "the customer comes first," but his boss has made such an issue of "policy" that Ted is afraid to break the rules. When managers set down inflexible rules, are they working with their staff members or controlling them? When managers control their employees, service often goes down the tubes — along with staff morale!

> *When managers control their employees, service often goes down the tubes.*

3. Confidence-building

Let the people on your team know you believe in them and in what they're doing. Point to past successes ... to their individual and team accomplishments. Review with them the keys to those successes and praise the commitment to excellence behind each victory.

One way to do this is to publish a regular list of individual and team accomplishments over the past week or month. Make sure the list is posted in a visible area or incorporated into a simple newsletter distributed to your team members and other key organizational people. Such a tool accomplishes three things:

- It lets team members know you are aware of their efforts to excel.

- It provides "performance exposure" for members within and beyond the team environment.

- It encourages a healthy competitive desire to "make the list" and go the extra mile.

Let people know you know they can do the job and you'll see something wonderful happen: They'll start to get confidence in themselves. They'll start to believe in themselves and accomplish more than even they thought they could.

4. Mutuality

Mutuality means sharing a vision of common goals. If you as a leader have goals that head one way and your people have goals heading another, the team will fall apart. All too often employees (and sometimes managers) don't have clear-cut goals.

To make sure your team goals are "mutual" — shared by every member — you must take the time to explain your goals in detail. Make sure your team members can answer questions like: *Why is this goal good for the team? For the organization? How will it benefit individual members? What steps must be taken to achieve the goal? When? What rewards can we expect when the goal is achieved?*

Here's a good example of a goal in memo form that answers
all the questions on the previous page.

Clarity of the task

Timelines defined

Mutuality

Benefits to staff

Benefits to organization

Dear Team:

As you know, the warehouse full of new stock we
acquired from the recent merger has never been
inventoried. The Board has asked that we conduct an
inventory as soon as possible without affecting our
production schedule.

So I propose an inventory on the first and third
Saturdays of next month from 10 a.m. to 3 p.m. Eight
of us should be able to do the entire inventory in that
time frame — with time out for company-paid lunches!
Attendance isn't mandatory. No pressure. But I would
rather not hire temporaries to do this because the funds
will have to come from our miscellaneous funds
(summer picnic, company nights at the ballpark, etc.).

The proposed inventory schedule allows participants to
sleep late on Saturday and leave early enough to have
some R&R. Also, volunteers will receive time-and-a-half
pay, plus one Friday off between now and Christmas.
When this inventory is finished, the Board estimates
that the company could see a 5-percent to 6-percent
increase in sales and that our production load for the
holidays will be significantly less!

Sign-up sheet is on the bulletin board. To join the fun
for one or both Saturdays, you must sign before Friday
at 5 p.m.

See you there!

Clay

Without goals, mutuality is impossible. You and your team
won't go anywhere special. With goals, you are destined for
greatness!

5. Perspective

Psychologist George Kelly calls perspective "understanding from the inside out." It's getting inside a person and seeing things from his perspective. Looking at people from the outside in too often results in labeling them. Do you have words and names for people who work for you? Little terms you use to describe them, sometimes? Grumpy ... Johnny-Come-Lately ... The Complainer ... etc.? When we do that, we're understanding people from the outside in instead of the inside out. That means we probably don't understand them at all.

To understand someone from the inside out, you have to ask questions:

> **What's new in your life, Paul?**
>
> **Anything I could do to make it easier for you to complete this project? (or be at work on time? or feel better about your assignment? etc.)**
>
> **Why don't we have lunch, Alice, and get caught up on how things are going?**

These kinds of get-involved questions can ultimately reveal who your team members really are. They often disclose medical or family struggles that would make anyone "grumpy" — especially if the boss cares little about employee life beyond the office. These questions reveal the reasons why Johnny comes late and the complainer complains ... reasons for which you might spot obvious and immediate remedies!

For instance, if project delays spring from uncertainties about how to do the job, you might schedule training to provide needed skills and confidence.

If tardiness is the result of having no money to fix an ailing car, you might recommend some creative ways the employee could earn extra dollars, or ask personnel for a list of carpools near the employee's home.

To understand someone from the inside out, you have to ask questions.

If the employee feels resentful about unpleasant job assignments, you might explain in detail the need for the assignment and/or rotate the task between two or more employees.

The more questions you ask, the more you will understand what's going on inside your people. Don't assume that you know what they're thinking and feeling — ask them!

6. Risk

Risk is letting team members know it's OK to fail. The only way you can grow is by taking risks. Some people who work on your team may do nothing because they're afraid — afraid that if they take a risk and fail, you'll be upset. As you learned earlier, to be an effective coach you must communicate that *failure is not terminal, as long as everyone learns from it!* That's the key. Establish a clear, unthreatening way to deal with errors ... a way that starts with the individual. Such a process might have five key steps:

- Outline the specifics of the error with the employees concerned, asking for their help with the details.

- Identify the cause-and-effect principle involved (what was the domino that, when pushed, started the process necessary for the error to occur?).

- Determine at least two ways the same error could always be avoided.

- Agree on one measurable step (one you can check periodically) that the employees involved will take to avoid making the same error again.

- Determine logical rewards for correcting the behavior — as well as the exact consequences of continued failure to correct the error.

The only way you can grow is by taking risks.

Example:

Employee #1/Bob:
There's no getting around it. We let a typographical error get by in the Annual Report, and all 10,000 are printed already.

Coach/Kathleen:
How was that missed in the proofreading phase?

Employee #2/Karen:
Well, because the schedule was so tight, we only spell-checked it through the computer. One of us usually does a final proof, and that didn't happen. So instead of the word "sales," we typed the word "sale." The computer can't tell that's not a correct word.

Kathleen:
So we skipped a needed project phase to meet the project deadline?

Both:
Yes.

Kathleen:
How do you think we can avoid this with upcoming projects?

Karen:
I think we need a "check-off" system requiring verification of each phase before the job can move to the next one.

Bob:
That would work. Two of us could do a final proof on critical print projects. Some external projects like the Annual Report might warrant that.

Kathleen:
Those both sound like great ideas. Karen, could you sketch up what one of those "check-off" forms might look like?

Karen:
Sure.

If you never make mistakes, you'll never make discoveries.

Kathleen:
I'll take it with me when I tell Mr. Wells about the mistake. He isn't going to like this, but I think he will appreciate knowing we are taking concrete steps to avoid future errors.

If we can't avoid them, we might need to hire someone to do nothing but proofread, and there probably wouldn't be enough money in the budget to do that and still have Christmas bonuses.

Most successful people in this world have failed, are failing and will fail again. In a very real sense, it's smart to get excited about failures — because only through failures can you learn, grow and be better down the road.

7. Patience

Most of us hate patience. It's the "P" word. The "P" word goes with the "T" word: time. Yet time is a healer. Every successful StaffCoach™ knows that time and patience are the keys to preventing a manager from simply "reacting." Sure, there are times when emergency, on-the-spot decisions must be made:

- *When the refrigerated truck carrying your frozen food shipment breaks down somewhere between Fallon and Reno, Nev.*

- *When a client calls with a great job that's so big it could tax your ability to deliver on time — and if he can't get your answer now, the job will go to someone else.*

- *When the press is ready to roll, and you must either approve the colors on the press or get verification by the boss — which would cause you to miss your deadline.*

But most managers confirm that such times are surprisingly rare. And even those emergency situations almost always allow you time to ask for a quick word of advice or insight from a respected peer or supervisor.

> *"Crisis doesn't make or break you — it reveals you."*
>
> *— Don Moomaw*

13

Generally, a coach can and should avoid knee-jerk responses to unexpected situations; this type of reaction can undermine your associates' confidence and ability to think and react. Build some time between the event and your response to it. Use this time to:

- Evaluate the situation objectively — write it down if possible.

- Identify alternative solutions with pros and cons for each.

- Get respected opinions and input.

- Implement your chosen response.

- Assess results and alter your approach as needed.

The best StaffCoaches™ don't react — they act. They use patience to their advantage.

8. Involvement

Involvement means caring for someone enough to attempt to understand his experiences. It's getting out from behind your desk and going to where your staff is. It's finding out what's going on with your people. It's being interested enough to find out the significant facts about family background, ethnic origins, special hardship situations, ambitions and drive — as well as what type of person the employee is: shy, outgoing, easy to please, suspicious, etc.

For example, hearing that one of your foremen will soon be a new father can help explain his recent absent-mindedness. But taking *extra* time to know him better will alert you that the child his wife miscarried several years ago had Down's syndrome. His concerns, therefore, go deeper than mere nervousness and could result in major errors — maybe even an extended absence.

Not only does coach involvement confirm your genuine concern for team members as valuable human beings, it is also the key element in developing employee loyalty and helping you know how to motivate each unique team member.

9. Confidentiality

Confidentiality results when people demonstrate the rare ability to keep quiet. Some managers talk when they should be silent — often to prove (usually to themselves) that they are in a position of power. The most successful leaders are those who can keep their mouths shut. It takes discipline to stop yourself and not give away confidences. The moment you betray a confidence, trust is lost. And once you lose an employee's trust, it's almost impossible to get it back.

For instance, a manager discovered (through individual performance-appraisal discussions) that two of his employees shared the problem of having alcoholic spouses. Thinking the two might be encouraged by knowing that fact about each other, the manager shared the news with one of them. When the second employee discovered that someone else knew about her husband's problem, she resigned immediately. Moral? Even when sharing confidential information might seem justified, it isn't.

10. Respect

Respect involves a manager's *perceived* attitude toward the individuals he leads. You may respect your team members highly, but if they don't perceive that value ... if it is contradicted by your failure to share goals, your unwillingness to become involved, your inability to exercise patience ... you communicate disrespect. How far do you think a team can go together if its members feel the coach disdains them? If you answered "nowhere," you're right!

Once you lose an employee's trust, it's almost impossible to get it back.

CASE STUDY

Ben Anderson is the creative director for a growing advertising agency. The agency's three key accounts have requested urgent attention to large and unexpected projects — each of which is due about the same time.

After discussing the situation with the agency president, Ben calls a Friday morning meeting with his art directors, his copy chiefs and the account executives for each of the three projects. In that meeting, Ben asks each account executive to explain the project needs and goals and answer any questions Ben's key people might have. After the meeting, Ben orders in pizza and spends the rest of the afternoon with his leadership team, brainstorming scheduling options, personnel requirements and potential stumbling blocks to meeting the triple deadline.

On Monday morning, Ben calls a meeting of the entire 17-person creative department, in which he announces the upcoming projects. He introduces the three creative directors who will head each project, who in turn outline their project specifics ... the teams selected for each ... as well as the projected timetables.

Ben closes the hour-long meeting by distributing a handout outlining and discussing the goals of each project and its benefits to the agency, as well as announcing the department "awards" picnic that will take place when the projects are completed.

Over the next five weeks of project activity, Ben meets regularly with each project leader and account executive to review progress and any special challenges or difficulties. He attends weekly team meetings, where project leaders and team members on each of the three projects evaluate completed project phases and anticipate possible problems.

When one of the computer illustrators becomes ill, Ben fills in for him until he can return two days later.

As the project deadlines approach, Ben's project leaders recommend hiring two temporary graphics people for one day. Ben agrees. When the three projects are finally completed and approved, one project comes in two days early, one is right on time, and one is a half day late. None of the other projects in the agency's system have fallen behind during that time.

Each team member receives a questionnaire asking what he felt went right about each project, what went wrong and how the problems can be avoided next time. Results of the questionnaires are studied and compiled into a full report available to all participants.

To the department picnic for team members and their families, Ben invites client representatives who speak to the group expressing gratitude and pleasure with project results. Plaques are awarded to each department member for "Most Paranoid" ... "Most Oblivious to Pain" ... "Most Motivated by Food," etc. And as Ben wraps things up with a few closing remarks, his project leaders dump a cooler of Gatorade on his head.

CASE STUDY ANALYSIS

1. Listed below are the 10 values of a successful StaffCoach™. Beside each, note how Ben Anderson exhibited or failed to exhibit the value listed.

    Clarity:

    Supportiveness:

    Confidence-building:

    Mutuality:

17

CASE STUDY ANALYSIS

Perspective:

Risk:

Patience:

Involvement:

Confidentiality:

Respect:

2. How do you think members of the department felt about Ben's attitude toward the tasks? Toward them?

3. What do you think was the key to Ben's success? How could that key ingredient help you in the next three months?

4. How would your team members feel about working for someone like Ben? Why?

5. What would you have done differently from Ben? Why?

CASE SUMMARY

Ben's ability to adequately direct the business needs of several key customers while not overwhelming his staff is truly evident in this case. Many people would jump into the projects anticipating overload without a plan. The fact that Ben planned before he acted is a contributing factor in the success. Planning early in a project is never wasted; planning early in a project and then effectively communicating to your staff can be taken to the bank (which is one of the strengths of Ben's actions). Although not overly emphasized in this case, there appears to be considerable involvement of Ben's team and appropriate incentives established for hard and effective work. Ben's team knew the workload demand was heavy but there was a company picnic to mark the end. People are much more willing to go above and beyond when they know there is an end in sight.

One last point that's worth mentioning is the humorous awards presented at the picnic. Although we can only speculate from the case, there appears to be a sense of fun. That's often an uncommon feature during project crunch time. Any coach who makes the work bearable should be applauded, but when the team can laugh and have fun along the way, the coach is "Super-Bowl potential."

WHAT YOU VALUE WILL IMPACT YOUR TEAM

Managers are too often unaware of the impact their values have on other people's lives. The truth is, every day you imprint your values upon your team.

Ask yourself this question: "What kinds of values and attitudes do I communicate to the team I lead?" An attitude of supportiveness, confidence, commitment, mutuality, patience and involvement? Which value or values do you need to add? To eliminate? To answer those questions, it is often helpful to identify where your attitudes come from.

Have you ever thought about where you got your values? As you were maturing, there were people who influenced you, who helped you become who you are today. Usually those people inspired, taught or corrected you.

In your early years, your parents, teachers and siblings were probably the people who inspired you ... challenged you to go further, dream bigger, reach higher. They were also the people who taught you ... helped you understand the relationship between cause and effect, imparted a desire for knowledge, independence, etc. And of course they corrected you. In your middle years, usually the people who inspired you were friends ... maybe people from your church or public figures. Your spouse may have inspired you ... maybe

Along the way, someone has made a significant and positive difference in your values.

19

successful athletes … maybe a boss or co-worker. Maybe even a drill instructor!

How about the people who corrected you (reprimanded, redirected, disciplined, etc.)? Besides the other influences listed, some people list *themselves* — and, in fact, the older we grow, the more we see our *mature self* doing much of the teaching and correcting we need!

Anyone reading this book could probably tell a story about a person from the past who has made an impact on his life. Along the way, someone has made a significant and positive difference in your values. Here is an exercise designed to help you pinpoint those relationships and the values you gained from them.

Tracing Your Personal Values History

	1 AGE __ to __			2 AGE __ to __			3 AGE __ to __		
	NAME	POS VALUE	NEG VALUE	NAME	POS VALUE	NEG VALUE	NAME	POS VALUE	NEG VALUE
INSPIRERS									
TEACHERS									
CORRECTORS									

Directions:

Divide your age into thirds and put those thirds in the three numbered blanks at the top of the chart shown here. For example, if you are 45, write 1-15 in the first blank. In the second blank write 16-30; and in blank three, write 31-45. It doesn't have to be exact. You can round off the numbers.

Now go to the square on the left side that says "Inspirers." To the right of that square, write the names of three people who inspired you in your early years. Move to Column 2 (your middle years) and do the same thing. Then do the same for your later years in Column 3.

Next, move to "Teachers" and repeat that process. Think of three people who were your role models. Then drop to the bottom of the chart and list three people who corrected you — three people who said "Yes" and "No." If you can't think of three names each time, don't worry. As you continue through this manual, other people will come to mind who relate to this exercise. You can return to this page and jot the name.

Now, in the blocks titled "Positive Values" and "Negative Values," write down the attitudes, ideas or goals that each person you listed communicated to you — the teacher who acted as a coach and especially inspired you ... the parent who challenged you to go "above and beyond."

For example, your first column might list "Mom" and "Junior High Principal" as two key figures who provided life inspiration during the first third of your life. Positive inspirational values that Mom imparted might include "persistence." Negative values might include "critical of others." The school principal may have inspired you to "aim high," while on the negative side, he may have communicated a tendency toward "perfectionism"... a feeling that becoming anything less than a brain surgeon was not a real job.

Did someone touch your inner chords and help you develop skills that perhaps even you didn't know you had? Remember those people who especially inspired, taught and corrected you, and the attitudes they had that you admired. Are these attitudes you communicate to others daily?

**E
X
E
R
C
I
S
E**

NOW WHAT?

Did you discover some things about yourself? If nothing else, isn't it surprising how significantly others can impact our lives? That's exactly the effect you are having on every one of your team members every day.

Now, based on your past managerial experience and on the values you just identified as being true of yourself, review the "10 Values of a Successful StaffCoach™" discussed earlier and listed here. Place an "X" after each value in the most appropriate column.

	I demonstrate these StaffCoach™ values:				
	Always	*Usually*	*Sometimes*	*Rarely*	*Never*
1. **Clarity**					
2. **Supportiveness**					
3. **Confidence-building**					
4. **Mutuality**					
5. **Perspective**					
6. **Risk**					
7. **Patience**					
8. **Involvement**					
9. **Confidentiality**					
10. **Respect**					

If you are like the vast majority of managers seeking to improve their leadership skills, this exercise will reveal some good news and ... well ... some not-so-good news. But either one is good! *Knowing what must be done is the essential first step toward doing it.* The checklists, exercises, self-tests and other tools in this book are assembled especially to help you see measurable growth in any value area you want to improve. If you doubt that, try this same exercise again 30 days after you have applied the principles you are about to learn. You (and your team members) will be delighted.

At the beginning of this chapter you read that great coaches aren't born, they are developed. In a real sense, they are "self-made" men and women. Using the tools outlined in this book will help you "make" yourself, too!

FIVE INSIGHTS OF HIGH-PERFORMANCE COACHES

No coach has ever had the "perfect team." The best teams you've ever seen — the ones you may have wished you had — all have their share of personality types that could drive anyone crazy. The difference between the success and failure of any team is how well the coach understands its members and motivates them.

> *No coach has ever had the "perfect team."*

To make that happen, a coach must possess five high-performance insights:

1. People reflect their views of life.

2. Individuality should be valued and explored.

3. Lack of motivation often reflects discouragement.

4. Consequences determine performance.

5. People treated responsibly *take responsibility.*

Let's review each of these insights in detail.

1. People reflect their views of life.

If you have an employee who is negative and pessimistic ... grumbling and complaining all the time ... you can predict exactly how he views life. Negatively. If an employee is generally happy and sees problems as challenges, you can pretty well count on that person having a positive outlook on life.

As a StaffCoach™, you need to understand the philosophies of the people who work for you.

Those philosophies, conscious and unconscious, include:

- Work is what I do to fund my weekends.

- If life gives you lemons, make lemonade.

- This job is a rung on my ladder to success.

- No one can do everything, but everyone can do something.

- Humor: Don't leave home without it.

- Whatever's wrong, I didn't do it.

- Know your limits, then break through them.

- If you learn from losing, you're a winner.

Recognize anyone you know? In some cases you may need to help team members rewrite those philosophies. How? If a very negative or uncommunicative person works for you, your natural reaction is to avoid that person. But as a coach, you'll never understand what makes that employee tick unless you spend time with him. You have to get close enough to understand the person's attitude or action.

For instance, negative people sometimes develop outward attitudes to mask inner feelings of inferiority. Make sure they believe *you* feel they are capable, valuable team members.

Some minds are like concrete — all mixed up and permanently set!

Coach:
You know, Jeff, I've been thinking about what you said about that last project being a waste of time, and I think you may have had a point.

Jeff:
About what?

Coach:
We *do* waste a lot of time around here sometimes. I think the newer people would really benefit from your experience identifying those time wasters.

Jeff:
What do you mean?

Coach:
I was hoping you would consider doing a short presentation on how to plan effectively for a project. After all, no one knows how better than you.

Helping an employee develop a positive perspective is essential, but be honest in your methods. Don't make up affirming things to say about an employee. But don't be afraid to challenge the employee's attitudes with additional job involvement. The result can mean new levels of productivity.

2. Individuality should be valued and explored.

Too many leaders don't allow their people to be unique and creative. Instead, they distrust individuality and smother the people on their team. They want a team of clones — people who respond to every situation just as they would. That's not coaching — and it's not how you get the best out of your team.

Each of the people on your team has unique capabilities and creative resources. If you have five team members, you have five creative resources besides your own. How do you know what those unique gifts are? Assuming your team is fairly new, you could ask the people your team members have worked for previously. You could review team members' original resumes, job applications and/or performance reviews. Or you could just ask them!

Too many leaders want a team of clones.

25

One way to ask them directly is through an informal questionnaire. While you will want to tailor this tool to your specific needs, a generic *Talent Inventory* might include questions like:

- What are your special job strengths as a member of our team?

- What would you say your weaker areas might be?

- If you were tackling a project (name a project relative to your environment), what responsibilities would you enjoy most? Which would you feel most qualified for? Least qualified?

- If your team could know only one thing about you, what should that one thing be?

- If you could expand your knowledge and skill level in any area of our duties as a team, what area would you like that to be?

Working together will naturally reveal more about the talents and potentials of your entire team, but little tools like the previous questionnaire can help greatly. You may discover that Jane can supervise projects. Joe has a knack for details, etc. When you start tapping the creativity and uniqueness of the people on your team, you create a dynamic called "synergy." The creativity of each member contributes to the creativity of the group, becoming something greater than you or any one individual could contribute.

It is helpful in grasping this concept to think of the words "symphony" and "energy" coming together in one word — "synergy." It's as if you are a conductor, coaxing the individual notes (energy) from each person who contributes to the whole (symphony). Don't be a boss who thinks that everyone has to conform — who is threatened by or distrustful of the creativity of the group.

Let your people express their individuality within the project framework.

26

Team members who excel in the organizational aspects of a task should ideally be involved in planning, scheduling, tracking, etc. Team members whose talents are primarily creative might be involved in concept development and product refinement. Even when such specialization isn't possible ... when the job description does not fully reflect an employee's primary aptitude ... *be open to modifications that can benefit the team!* For instance, a person whose responsibilities are basically clerical might exercise creative talent by developing a team logo or banner as time permits. The point is, let your people express their individuality within the project framework. Not only will you see tremendous gains in productivity, but staff morale will increase dramatically, as well.

3. Lack of motivation often reflects discouragement.

When people are not motivated, it's often because they are discouraged, not because they are lazy or stupid or ill. Find out *why* they're discouraged. If you can identify that ... and then be creative in your encouragement ... the motivation you were missing can suddenly begin to resurface.

How do you find the reason for the discouragement? For starters, try the same source that told you about the problem in the first place. If the source isn't the individual in question, naturally you must verify the information with the team member personally. However, discouragement can show itself in many other ways: a decrease in productivity, less attention to detail, tardiness, absenteeism, etc.

Ultimately, a one-on-one "RAP" meeting is a good way to confront the problem. **RAP** is a widely used acronym that stands for:

> **R** eview the past
> **A** nalyze the present
> **P** lan the future

With this approach, you and the team member can focus on a review of past performance contrasted with present performance — and then look together to an improved future. This simple tool is logical and easy to remember. When the RAP approach is followed, most coaches have no difficulty

**R
A
P**

keeping track of where the meeting is going and what progress has already been made.

Another plus of the RAP model is the emphasis it puts on future solutions. Discussions of the past and present are much less important than planning for the future, especially since the goal is to help team members work more closely to their potential.

Coach:
Jenny, I really like the way your company newsletter has caught on and the way you are handling it along with all your other duties.

Jenny:
I enjoy it.

Coach:
I can tell! I don't know if you realize it or not, but you have averaged working about three more hours per week since you began doing this newsletter, and you haven't been late to work once in the last four weeks.

Jenny:
I knew I was probably working a little harder.

Coach:
You really are. I think you have solved the attendance problem we talked about last February. The newsletter idea was a great way to make use of your interests! Because you are so good at this and I believe this is a skill you can develop for the company's benefit as well, I would like to relieve you of one of your other responsibilities and delegate it to someone else.

Remember, the "P" in RAP makes the process work. Help your team members identify goals that excite them and maximize their capabilities.

4. Consequences determine performance.

The best way to change performance is to carry out appropriate consequences. Consequences are essential! If an employee constantly performs unsatisfactorily, examine the

The best way to change performance is to carry out appropriate consequences.

consequences of that behavior. If no negative consequences exist, guess what? The behavior will continue. And if no good or positive consequences exist for changing the behavior, guess what? No change. The consequences (negative or positive) must fit the behavior in order to change it — and they must be implemented immediately and consistently.

Example:

A group of businessmen in Olathe, Kan., decided they needed to lose weight. So they started a contest — the winner to be honored by the losers. However, half the men, recalling their past record of failure, decided to approach the weight loss a little differently. They elected to record each member's weight weekly. Any participant who did not lose at least 1 pound each week paid every member who *had* lost 1 pound $10. Which group do you suppose lost weight faster? You guessed it. When it comes to measurable change, consequences are king!

5. People treated responsibly take responsibility.

Team members who are viewed as responsible for their actions tend to take responsibility. Have you noticed that when someone gives you responsibility, you tend to rise to that level of trust? The same thing happens with the people on your team. As you give them responsibility, they will rise to it. And when you do that, you also help that team member develop pride, self-respect and loyalty!

If a member of your team performs unsatisfactorily, take a few minutes to review the Five Insights of High-Performance Coaches. Usually, the key to the person's bad behavior and the remedy to the problem lie in one of these five essential insights!

CASE STUDY

Jennifer and Paul recently assumed StaffCoaching™ roles in the same division of a large greeting card firm. Both were supervisors before their promotions. Both wrote down their plans as new StaffCoaches™ for their respective departments.

C
A
S
E

S
T
U
D
Y

Jennifer said she looked forward to defining the Calendar and Album development challenges her team faced and then providing the team with well-defined goals and standards. Because of her job knowledge, she also planned to prepare a detailed performance model for each employee. She felt this approach would assure consistency in goals and performance standards and would measure job and performance progress.

Paul said he had enrolled in a management-skills seminar to make sure he understood the coaching process. In the meantime, he planned to involve his Notes and Stationery group in day-to-day planning, organizing and problem-solving. He felt his job experience was a strong plus but wanted every member of his team to contribute to the group's effectiveness. Paul also said that team members need the growth that comes from being involved in a project.

Which of these StaffCoaches™ would you like to work for? Why?

ANALYSIS

Jennifer and Paul both recognize the importanceJ of goals and plans. Employees who have limited knowledge or experience may appreciate Jennifer's approach because they have more to learn. Her standards and models will provide needed guidance. As they learn under her coaching style, however, they may soon feel reluctant to share their own job ideas. New work methods plus simpler and better ways to achieve objectives might be rare under Jennifer's leadership. Experienced employees may feel an immediate sense of confinement.

Experienced employees will appreciate Paul's approach, because it provides a needed outlet for involvement. They will feel free to contribute to the team's effectiveness while working on their own. Employees with lesser skills will feel encouraged to learn, so they too can become more productive and contribute. Paul's team will respect his decision to participate in StaffCoach™ training, seeing it as a willingness to commit to and invest in each team member.

"If you want to be in the 'trained-seal' business, get a job in the zoo."

— Chuck Knox

30

CHAPTER QUIZ

1. What does "management" mean?

2. Why are people "unlimited resources"?

3. Name the 10 values of a successful StaffCoach™.

4. What does the acronym RAP mean?

5. Name one way you can better understand the unique talents and abilities of each team member.

The Five-Step StaffCoaching™ Model

"Success is not established by how high we climb as managers, but by how many people we take with us as we climb."
— Bob Norton

A PERFORMANCE PROCESS THAT STARTS RIGHT WHERE YOU ARE!

You have learned the 10 values successful StaffCoaches™ share — values that enhance their interaction with team members, that enhance team member response to their leadership and that generate desired performance and productivity. You've learned some of the insights you need to have as a StaffCoach™ who wants every team member to realize her potential for individual growth, team success and project excellence. Now you're ready to begin exploring ways these leadership values and insights can impact your team and tasks more meaningfully.

Key to beginning that process is understanding a basic but universal truth:

No matter where you are, no matter how many people you put together on a team, you will always experience the same phenomenon: Some team members will perform above

> *Bob Norton considers himself to be a people person whose ambition in life is to help people grow and learn. He holds a bachelor's degree in communications from Azusa Pacific University and is a training specialist in a number of areas, including administration, communication, marketing, negotiation and conflict management. His business experience ranges from being vice president of a land development company to manager of a thriving California country club to consultant.*

**E
X
E
R
C
I
S
E**

expectations ... some will perform at an average or standard level ... and some will perform at substandard levels.

As a successful StaffCoach™, you must deal with each of these performance levels differently — and that's what the Five-Step StaffCoaching™ Model is all about. The Five-Step StaffCoaching™ Model is a highly effective framework that provides managers with proven techniques for achieving greater results from their people.

To implement this simple but powerful model, the first thing you must assess is the current performance level of each team member. What are the standards for each person's performance? Is the person you're dealing with performing above the standard, working at the standard level or performing below standard?

One helpful way to arrive at answers to these essential beginning questions is to compile information about each team member on a form like the one shown here. It doesn't have to be a complicated form. It isn't intended to function as a formal Performance Evaluation Report — only as a worksheet for establishing initial leadership direction.

Performance Assessment

Name _____

Basic Responsibilities	Obvious Strengths	Obvious Weaknesses	Overall Assessment Of Performance Historically (Superior, Average Substandard)	Performance During Last Year	Immediate StaffCoach™ Action

Once you have clearly identified where each team member is in her individual development and how that performance impacts the team, you will be ready to move on with specific steps that maximize each team member's growth potential. The rest of this book will discuss those steps in detail.

Step 1. "Assess present performance" is where success starts, as you can see on the Five-Step StaffCoaching™ Model illustration shown at right. Once the employee's present performance level has been established, you are ready to (2) coach, (3) mentor or (4) counsel, as the situation warrants. As we will learn in subsequent chapters, steps 2 through 4 of the Five-Step StaffCoaching™ Model are applied as follows:

Step 2. If a person is achieving above-standard performance, you'll respond in the role of coach.

Step 3. For those delivering average or "standard" performance, you'll respond in the role of mentor.

Step 4. Team members operating below standard performance need your involvement in the role of counselor.

Step 5. This is the ongoing act of integrating each team member ... at whatever performance stage she exhibits ... into the team in a positive, productive and fulfilling role. But again, steps 2-5 will be thoroughly discussed in later chapters.

For now, let's start with Step No. 1: Identifying your team members' performance levels. How do you do that? How can you know if you are right?

> *The way to get anywhere is to start from where you are.*

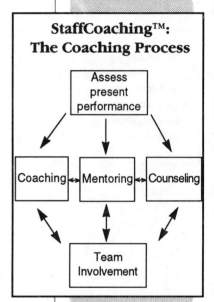

**StaffCoaching™:
The Coaching Process**

KNOWING YOUR EMPLOYEES' CHARACTER AND CAPABILITIES:
FOUR EFFECTIVE APPROACHES

I) Personal observation

By now it has probably become evident that StaffCoaching™ requires firsthand knowledge of, and one-on-one familiarity with, your team members and their jobs. There is no way around that. And a good StaffCoach™ doesn't *want* or look for a way around it. The better you know your people, the better you can make the right game-winning decisions in critical situations.

Not surprisingly, therefore, *assessing the performance levels of your team members starts with developing firsthand information about each person on the team.*

To cover all the bases, let's assume you are totally new to your team. You have just signed on and are ready to meet and evaluate team members. Let's further assume that you are already familiar with the overall team function and individual job descriptions that contribute to team success. How do you become familiar with each team member and how well she is doing the job at hand?

Undoubtedly you will have talked with your supervisors (if any) about personnel and job challenges as they perceive them. *But the task of evaluating an employee's performance does not start with other people. It starts with the team member.* Why? Because your own firsthand impressions and opinions are key to performance objectivity. The time will come when the thoughts of others can and should be weighed. But not before you have firsthand impressions of the personalities, problems and potentials that create your unique team mix.

> *The better you know your people, the better you can make the right game-winning decisions.*

The face-to-face phase

So, talk to your employee. Find a time when you are both free to spend at least 30 minutes to an hour in uninterrupted, casual conversation, and schedule a comfortable get-to-know-each-other chat. The goals of your time together will be three-fold.

To understand:

A.   **What motivates your employee**

B.   **What problems and pluses (professional and personal) she perceives about performing daily tasks**

C.   **What goals she has for career growth and development**

While insights into each of these areas could surface during random, undirected conversation, many managers have found that *asking nine specific questions usually achieves the three goals mentioned.* Naturally, you will want to modify these questions to better suit your own situation, but the nine questions are:

1.   **What do you like best about your job?**

2.   **What do you like least?**

3.   **What has satisfied you most about your job performance in recent months?**

4.   **What has frustrated you most about project duties?**

5.   **What is the thing you feel you contribute best as a member of our team?**

6.   **What changes have you recommended in your job over the past year?**

7.   **What training has best prepared you to do what you do?**

> *If you are a manager, even of insignificant things, you'll never be an insignificant manager.*

37

8. **Are there aspects of your job for which you feel unequipped in any way?**

9. **What is the one area of your job in which you would like to improve?**

Again, you will want to phrase these questions in a way that feels comfortable to you. But when they are asked during the employee/coach "face-to-face phase," the employee will usually give you the information you need to proceed to the next phase.

NOTE: Do not ask these questions from a list or make notes during your employee's responses. These questions should sound spontaneous and conversational. While it is natural that you should as a coach be asking the questions, it is not helpful to communicate the feeling that the team member is being graded on her responses. Immediately after the interview you can record your question-by-question impressions and recollections, but not during the interview.

Interview recap phase

In addition to recording concrete responses to the nine questions posed, it can also be helpful to record your impressions of the interview on a form that focuses on some of the more intuitive, subjective or abstract aspects of the meeting. Why? Because you are attempting to determine which StaffCoach™ approach each team member needs most: coaching, mentoring or counseling. *All* the data you can gather to help you help the employee in this regard should be considered. Toward that end, many coaches have found this post-interview form to be a valuable tool for assessing team-member development needs.

INTERVIEW RECAP FORM

Team Member Name _____   **Date** _____

	Not Evident								Very Evident
Commitment to job/ organization	1	2	3	4	5	6	7	8	9
People tolerance	1	2	3	4	5	6	7	8	9
Project tolerance	1	2	3	4	5	6	7	8	9
Self-starter	1	2	3	4	5	6	7	8	9
Desire to excel	1	2	3	4	5	6	7	8	9
Willingness to learn	1	2	3	4	5	6	7	8	9
Responsive to constructive criticism	1	2	3	4	5	6	7	8	9
Openness to new job direction	1	2	3	4	5	6	7	8	9
Self-confidence/esteem	1	2	3	4	5	6	7	8	9

Total _____

Add the numbers in each column and total them. A score of 27 or less probably indicates a need for counseling and/or mentoring in several areas. A score of 54 or less points to the likelihood of mentoring in several performance areas. A score of 63 or better indicates a primary need for coaching.

On-the-job contact

No firsthand picture of employee aptitude and performance would be complete without observation in the actual job setting. In some environments, this will be easier than in others. Evaluating an assembly line technician will be easier than evaluating, say, a writer. Or observing a CAD operator is easier than assessing a computer programmer. Nonetheless, your collective impressions from viewing each team member on the job will contribute to your overall assessment of that person's attitudes and aptitudes.

And what exactly are you looking for? Although the following checklist is very general, it should provide basic working guidelines for observing and evaluating members of your team.

ON-THE-JOB EVALUATION FORM

Team Member Name _____   **Date** _____

	Not Evident								Very Evident
On-the-job confidence	1	2	3	4	5	6	7	8	9
Tolerance for stress	1	2	3	4	5	6	7	8	9
Standards of Excellence	1	2	3	4	5	6	7	8	9
Attention to detail	1	2	3	4	5	6	7	8	9
Innovation	1	2	3	4	5	6	7	8	9
Flexibility/openness to alternatives	1	2	3	4	5	6	7	8	9
Ability to teach, model	1	2	3	4	5	6	7	8	9
Acceptance by peers/superiors	1	2	3	4	5	6	7	8	9
Speed	1	2	3	4	5	6	7	8	9

Total _____

41

Add the numbers in each column and total them. A score of 27 or less probably indicates a need for counseling and/or mentoring in several areas. A score of 54 or less points to the likelihood of mentoring in several performance areas. A score of 63 or better indicates a primary need for coaching.

II) Supervisory/Personnel Information

Assuming, as we are, that you are new to this team environment, the ability to obtain the evaluations and assessments of supervisors and/or personnel files will be very helpful in determining the performance level of your team members.

What are you looking for?

A. Performance reviews

Any insights and information you can gain from the recorded evaluations of previous managers will be helpful in gauging team-member problems or potential.

B. Supervisor insights

If your team is large enough to include supervisory personnel, then you should carefully evaluate their views and performance appraisals of team members' attitudes, aptitudes and actions at this point.

One way to standardize supervisory input to the performance-evaluation process is to employ a five-point form like the one shown on the next page. Each supervisor should be asked to complete one of these forms for each of the members on her team.

SUPERVISORY OBSERVATION FORM

1. **My overall impression of this employee's skill level relative to her job description is:**

2. **I believe this individual excels in:**

3. **This person needs to improve in:**

4. **My assessment of this person's professional improvement over the last one to two years is:**

5. **My recommendation for this employee in the immediate future is:**

III) Extra-Departmental Observations

If your team interacts regularly with other people, departments or divisions, the observations of selected professionals can often enlighten you about the perceived performance of your team members. Remember: The key word here is "perceived." The opinions of those who interact only *occasionally* with your people should be considered only as they support the overall weight of departmental opinion.

> **Note:** This method tends to be the *least* trustworthy way to assess a team member's performance level. Depending on your special situation, however, it can add some weight to your employee's performance appraisal.

IV) Team Member Input

Finally, understanding each team member's professional motivation, problems and career goals depends on having her input. While you have already conferred one-on-one with each team member, allowing each person to respond to a short informal questionnaire gives the employee the chance to amplify ideas she may have only touched on in your face-to-face interview. One such questionnaire ("Talent Inventory") was suggested in Chapter 1 (page 26). Here is another:

TEAM MEMBER QUESTIONNAIRE

1. **One of the ways I have felt most challenged in my job is:**

2. **One aspect of my job I have felt least inclined to perform is:**

    Because:

3. **If given the chance, I believe I can exceed my job requirements by:**

4. **One of the ongoing frustrations of my job is:**

5. **My professional goal is to:**

NOW WHAT?

Let's take a look at how you might arrive at a decision to tentatively place an employee in one of those three categories: coaching, mentoring or counseling. First review and analyze each of the written evaluation tools just discussed:

> *Interview Recap Form*
>
> *On-the-Job Evaluation Form*
>
> *Supervisory Observation Form*
>
> *Team Member Questionnaire*

Once you have completed the entire performance-evaluation process, you will have a good idea where each employee falls in the overall team picture. Obviously, your assessment isn't definitive, but you should know where to begin. Your evaluation of individual team members will change regularly as additional job performances are observed. Until then, your initial performance evaluation is a necessary step to help you encourage each employee to be the best she can be.

As we learned at the start of this chapter, some employees will be performing above expectations ... some at average or standard levels ... some at substandard levels. Some will be excellent at certain aspects of their jobs and substandard in other aspects.

It's difficult to analyze and evaluate the performance of an employee. You will undoubtedly find that each employee will have a mix of performance levels — each requiring a different StaffCoaching™ approach: counseling, mentoring and/or coaching.

Beginning in Chapter 3, we will learn about each of these StaffCoach™ options to team-member interaction — what they mean ... how they are done ... what they accomplish. But before that, we need to learn a little more about the person who will be implementing these StaffCoach™ techniques: **you**!

> *"Greatness lies not in being strong, but in the right use of strength."*
>
> *— Henry Ward Beecher*

> *"Every great work is at first impossible."*
>
> *— Thomas Carlyle*

WHAT'S YOUR STAFFCOACHING™ STYLE? AN INVENTORY THAT TELLS YOU

STAFFCOACHING™ STYLE INVENTORY

Supervisors and managers find themselves in critical incidents that require on-the-spot decisions. This inventory will help you identify your "StaffCoaching™ Style."

Rank your response to each situation, giving three (3) points for your top choice, two (2) for your second preference and one (1) for your least desired choice in each scenario.

1. Two employees in your department do not get along. One of them has asked you to intervene. You say …
   _____ a.   "Why should I get involved? You work it out, or come to me together."
   _____ b.   "I'll talk to the other party," thinking you'll get to the bottom of this before it gets out of hand.
   _____ c.   "Can you give me some background? Maybe we can work this out together."
2. During a staff meeting, one employee charges that your leadership efforts are a joke, that nothing gets done. After the meeting, you say …
   _____ a.   "Let's find out if everyone feels that way."
   _____ b.   "Let me state the goals of this project again."
   _____ c.   "I'm really concerned about your response; what do you mean?"
3. During a private conversation with another supervisor, you find out that his job may be eliminated. You say …
   _____ a.   "Let's explore the options available, O.K.?"
   _____ b.   Nothing, but probe to find out more information.
   _____ c.   "Do you want to talk about it?"
4. Personnel cuts must be made in your department. A meeting has been planned to announce the cuts, but another manager has cold feet and may not show up for the meeting. You say …
   _____ a.   "I understand your concern about giving bad news, but we're expected in this meeting. Let's look at some ways we can do this together."
   _____ b.   "You've got to be there. Think of the long-term reactions if you're not."
   _____ c.   "What do you think we can do so it's easier on both of us?"
5. You are assigning work responsibilities and identify a major conflict in the work priorities of an employee on your team. You say …
   _____ a.   "I really respect your thoughts and feelings on this. Let's talk about priorities."
   _____ b.   "I've got the jobs pretty well assigned and can't switch now. You've got to change what you're doing."
   _____ c.   "There's a logical way to meet both our goals. Let's see if we can find mutual priorities."
6. Your manager has called you to her office and asked your opinion on an employee who is not in your department. You say …
   _____ a.   "Can we talk about the goals and objectives before I give any opinions?"
   _____ b.   "You're talking to the wrong person."
   _____ c.   "I'm really glad you are checking out our employees; let me tell you what I think."
7. A major deadline is about to expire on one of your best accounts. You need every resource to meet the deadline, but one employee is very upset over family problems. You say …
   _____ a.   "Let's work together; this project must get out the door."
   _____ b.   "The show must go on; you'll have to leave personal business at home."
   _____ c.   "I'll call the client and see if I can get an extension for your part of the project."

STAFFCOACHING™ STYLE INVENTORY (Continued)

8. Every person in your unit has complained about the work of one person. In a team meeting, you have asked for feedback that would help the team, but no one speaks up. You say ...

   _____ a.   "We must get past the problems, so I'll start, but I expect the rest of you to join in."

   _____ b.   "This is bull! I know there are problems. Who's going to speak up?"

   _____ c.   Light-heartedly, "I guess there are no problems. I'll move on if no one says anything."

9. Over the past few weeks, it seems that employees have consistently ganged up on one worker. Every staff meeting is attack time. You say to the employee ...

   _____ a.   "I think you need to develop a strategy for getting through those attacks."

   _____ b.   "Why don't you speak up? What do you need right now?"

   _____ c.   "You don't have to be the target, unless you want to. You must really feel under attack. Let's find some way to stop the attack."

10. Projects are way behind and during a problem-solving session, one member begins to cry. You say ...

   _____ a.   "Let's take a break," thinking you can work with the person and allow time to recover.

   _____ b.   "I understand why you're upset."

   _____ c.   "Let's look at this together and see how to get out of this mess."

Scoring: Add up the columns. Now, starting on the left side, write in the far left box the word "Coach." In the middle box, put the word "Mentor," and in the box at the right, put the word "Counselor." Your highest score will tell you what your primary strength is likely to be. You should also look at your lowest score — that's where you are probably weak.

1. a. _____	c. _____	b. _____
2. c. _____	b. _____	a. _____
3. a. _____	b. _____	c. _____
4. c. _____	a. _____	b. _____
5. a. _____	c. _____	b. _____
6. c. _____	a. _____	b. _____
7. a. _____	b. _____	c. _____
8. c. _____	b. _____	a. _____
9. a. _____	b. _____	c. _____
10. c. _____	b. _____	a. _____

TOTAL _____   **TOTAL** _____   **TOTAL** _____

SO WHAT?

What difference does it make whether or not you are stronger or weaker in any of these areas? Good question. In the sense that none of the three areas is superior to the other, the answer is none at all. But knowing your stylistic tendencies as a StaffCoach™ can help you:

1. **Overcome natural inclinations to use a style you prefer but that may not meet an employee's immediate needs**
2. **Understand which StaffCoach™ style will require additional effort and study on your part (to be discussed) if you are to provide balanced leadership**

Most managers are strongest in counseling skills. That's because most of the time managers correct others. Most managers are weakest in mentoring. The reason? Mentoring takes two things: the "P" word and the "T" word. Patience and time — two commodities that managers (and professionals in general) find increasingly difficult to spare.

But as difficult as patience and time are to come by, failure to invest them in your employees will create pitfalls to success that can be extremely difficult to overcome. This brings us to the next important item in preparing you for StaffCoaching™ excellence.

SIX PITFALLS TO YOUR STAFFCOACHING™ SUCCESS

Let's pretend for a moment. Pretend that instead of wanting to be a motivational coach who inspires others to do their best, you want to undermine the team. You want the team to fail. Ridiculous, you say? Unfortunately, it happens every day. It's not that managers consciously want their teams to fail. It's just that without thinking, they do things that would defeat any team.

Most managers are strongest in counseling skills and weakest in mentoring.

Here are six approaches practically guaranteed to demoralize your people and keep them from reaching their goals.

1. **Talk at your employees, not with them.**
2. **Exaggerate situations or behavior.**
3. **Talk about attitudes rather than behavior.**
4. **Assume the employee knows the problem and solution.**
5. **Never follow up.**
6. **Don't reward improved behavior.**

1. Talk *at* your employees, not *with* them.

This killing tendency is all too common. When you talk *at* someone, you're talking down to her. You're being condescending. Often this kind of approach is accompanied by a pointing finger or pen, and the frequent use of words like "I want" and "you should." It can't even be called "giving orders" — it is attacking people with rank and the threat of retribution. The result? Over time, team members will either leave or, perhaps worse, gradually become what your tyrannical style is teaching them to be: responsive only to direct orders ... not self-starters ... distrustful of management ... uncommitted to your vision ... unmotivated to operate beyond performance minimums.

Managers should talk *with* team members. One of the best ways to do this is to start using the words "we," "our" and "us."

> *"We've got our work cut out for us in order to make the deadline we committed to."*

> *"Well, we blew it on that order. Let's figure out what we learned and do our best not to repeat the error."*

Collective pronouns communicate a subconscious sense of "team" that can make the most difficult news or the most challenging directions somehow less threatening or less overwhelming. The secret lies in your "team talk" as a coach.

Managers should talk with team members — not at them.

49

No one is "always" anything.

2. Exaggerate situations or behavior.

When you correct behavior using words like "always," "never," "all the time" and "everybody," you automatically drag people down. Generalizations attack the self-esteem of the individual. If you tell someone, "You're always late" or "You never do this" or "Everyone feels this way," you aren't telling the truth! No one is "always" *anything*. The moment you use "absolute" words your employee feels attacked. Instead of generalizations, be specific — and remember that your role of authority calls for insight ... not insensitivity!

3. Talk about attitudes rather than behavior.

When you criticize attitudes rather than behavior, you're begging for a defeated team. Have you heard something like this in a performance review? "You do this really well, and I appreciate what you're doing here, but the problem I see is your attitude."

When you say something like that to an employee, you attack self-esteem. A person's attitude is attached to who she is. You say, "Pat, you have a bad attitude," and in Pat's brain it translates to, "Pat, you are a bad person." No — you didn't say that, but that's what Pat hears. Think about it. If someone says to you, "Work on your attitude," what is your internal response? You become defensive, don't you? If you want openness between you and the people on your team, stop talking about attitudes. Instead, talk about behavior. If you want to change attitudes, that's where to start. Why? Because you can't modify other people's attitudes. You can only modify behavior.

> *"All we pay for every week*
> *is a certain kind of behavior for a*
> *certain amount of hours*
> *and that's the only thing we can modify."*
>
> *— Ferdinand Fournies*

4. Assume the employee knows the problem and solution.

If you assume the employee knows both the problem and the solution, you're definitely going to hurt the performance of your team. Assuming invariably costs time, money and morale. If you *must* assume something, always assume that your communications were somehow inadequate the first time. Then follow the ABCs of ensuring understanding:

Ask the employee what she thinks you want or said.

Blame no one if that understanding is wrong.

Communicate more clearly ... then confirm comprehension.

5. Never follow up.

If you fail to follow up on directions or performance, you will inevitably find yourself reacting to unpleasant surprises.

Example: Let's say you gave an assignment to someone on Monday, and it's due on Friday. You say, "I need this on Friday morning for a meeting." Friday morning comes and you ask the assigned person, "Where's that information you were going to give me this morning for the meeting?" The person looks at you and says, "I forgot" or "It's not done yet." If you're a yeller, you yell. If you're a crier, you cry. But who is really to blame? *You* are! You didn't follow up.

A crucial part of following up is setting objectives.

Example: You give someone an assignment on Monday morning. As you hand her the assignment you say, "By Wednesday, the first draft should be done. By Thursday, the rewritten version should be done, and by Friday, the whole thing should be completed." Then you follow up. You check on Wednesday to see if the project is on schedule. Then you check on Thursday. If for some reason

A
B
C

the project isn't where it's supposed to be, you and your employee can then:

- Pinpoint what is preventing project flow (job overload, lack of information, mind block, etc.)

- Eliminate the impediment (reassign conflicting work, brainstorm solutions, provide helpful materials, etc.)

- Determine how to get back on schedule (overtime? involvement of others? extended completion date?)

NOTE: Make sure you communicate that you're not doing this to control, but to help the responsible person get the best results.

"Let's just roll up our sleeves and tackle the problem together, Kristy. I know you are as eager as I am to do the project well, and I want to see you succeed."

Once you have implemented this procedure one or two times with a team member, watch her catch on and run with the ball on future projects!

6. Don't reward improved behavior.

If you don't reward positive changes in behavior, your team will be defeated. You will not gain *permanent* behavior changes. Every performance improvement, however small, deserves some type of reward. Behavioral scientist Frederick Hersberg studied motivation and discovered that *the top two things that motivate people are achievement and recognition.*

If people feel they're achieving something, they usually will be motivated. If you go through your day and feel as if you're getting nothing done, how do you feel at the end of that day? Frustrated. But if you go through your day and get a lot accomplished, you feel great! You're motivated. Similarly, when people are recognized for their achievements, they will be motivated. Take 10 to 20 minutes every week, at the end or

A crucial part of following up is setting objectives.

Every performance improvement, however small, deserves some type of reward.

the beginning, and sit down with your team. In that meeting, review what they've accomplished the last week. Recognize individuals. Tell them how much you appreciate what Gale has done or what Pat did today. When you do this, you're setting up your team to be motivated for the following week.

CASE STUDY

Raytown Kennels employs 12 people: one office manager, two clerical support people, two welders, two delivery people, two kennel maintenance people, one trainer, one veterinarian and one communications manager.

Bob Smith, the office manager, is also the owner of the business. Last fall, when the hunting season was in full swing, the business was faced with an unusually large demand for new kennels and dog houses. The welders could not keep up with requests.

Bob called a meeting and announced that everyone except the clerical support people would be taught how to construct kennels in two late-night training sessions. The welders were to provide the training. All were required to attend these sessions. No exceptions — because, as Bob put it, "The future of the business and everyone's job is on the line."

During the next 60 days, more than 30 kennel orders were filled on time. However, eight of them were returned or delivery was declined because of construction flaws or design errors. And the much-respected company veterinarian resigned to take a job with a competitor.

At a company picnic in the spring, Bob gave a short speech in which he thanked all in attendance for their loyalty during the last year and promised to avoid a repeat of "the fiasco of last fall" through better sales projections and production planning.

He closed by announcing that a new veterinary graduate would be joining the company in June.

C A S E S T U D Y

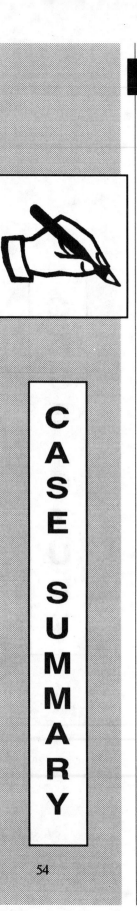

WHAT DO YOU THINK?

1. **What pitfalls to StaffCoaching™ success did Bob fall into?**

2. **What did he do right?**

3. **Briefly describe how Bob could have avoided the pitfalls you listed under No. 1.**

4. **If you were one of Bob's people, how would you feel about working for him?**

5. **What one thing could Bob do immediately to remedy the major problem(s) you see in his organization?**

CASE SUMMARY

Several things that could have been avoided seem to jump out of this case.

First, Bob did not have access to back-up staff or specialists that could meet his production demand. Although it seemed like a good idea to cross train his people in kennel making, the obvious dissatisfaction of some is noted. Bob could have avoided much of his difficulty by identifying free-lance welders or outside resources he could contact when welding demands rise. This also is a good idea to cover his delivery people and support staff. It is cost ineffective to have veterinary staff welding kennels or delivering products.

Second, the tone and atmosphere of Bob's decision seems questionable. Did his people enter into the plan? Were they willing volunteers meeting a business need or were they commanded to perform? Strong-arm tactics may lead to compliance but not necessarily quality work.

Third, Bob did not provide adequate incentive in the training. Reading the case makes an individual wonder why employees would give up their time and do work that is not within their job descriptions.

Last, Bob did not inspect or maintain any form of quality control, losing the most valuable resource he has, his customer loyalty. One alternative for Bob would have been to assign his welders as inspectors and quality-assurance monitors.

10 TOOLS FOR BUILDING A SOLID TEAM FOUNDATION

We have explored the hows and whys of identifying each of your employees' current performance levels. We've analyzed your StaffCoaching™ style to help you recognize your own areas of strength and possible weaknesses as a coach. We've examined the six common pitfalls to success that StaffCoaches™ face and how to sidestep them.

Now, before we begin studying the interaction roles in the Five-Step StaffCoaching™ Model, we must cover one more important element of successful StaffCoaching™: *how to build a solid team foundation.*

The following 10 key attributes of successful StaffCoaches™ help make the difference between good teams and great teams.

1. **Flexibility**
2. **Helping**
3. **Empathy and understanding**
4. **Valuing the employee**

5. **Listening**
6. **"Pro-active" mind-set**
7. **Effective feedback**
8. **Enthusiasm and optimism**
9. **Openness**
10. **Humor**

1. Flexibility

Have you been in your job more than two years? If so, chances are you're in a rut. It's true: People who have been in their jobs more than two years have a tendency toward laxity, lethargy ... toward "routine." And if you're stuck in a rut, it means you are probably more rigid in your leadership. The longer you're in a position, the more rigid you become ... the less flexible. And you may find yourself watching your team grow gradually less successful.

Every year, your team changes in some way. You need to grow with those changes. The most successful coaches are people who are flexible in responding to team development. They use different team strategies to succeed. What's an easy way to remain flexible? Be committed to personal growth. If you're going to be a flexible person, and especially a flexible leader, you've got to be committed to personal growth as a manager.

2. Helping

The willingness to work shoulder to shoulder with your team in accomplishing goals ... assisting in any way you can ... happens only as a result of your attitude. As the leader, you exist to help the people who work for you. That should be your professional mission. All too often, leaders don't think that way. They think that because they *are* leaders, their people are supposed to be helping them. Sorry. Not true. The true role of the successful coach is to assist members of her team to succeed in their efforts to further department and company goals.

The longer you're in a job, the more rigid you become.

Personal growth is the only guaranteed rut-preventer!

3. Empathy and understanding

To succeed as a coach, you must have empathy for the people who work for you — a basic understanding and acceptance of human nature. People are people. If you expect people to be super-beings or pawns in a corporate ladder-climbing game, you are in for a rude awakening. And your team is in for some very serious defeats.

To help you maintain a proper "people perspective," many managers have found these *"Five Golden Questions of Leading People"* to be helpful:

- Have I communicated the assignment in a way that makes my employee feel involved?

- Do my instructions provide helpful directions toward a mutually desired destination?

- Can my employee excel if she completes this assignment?

- If I had to perform this task I am assigning, would I look forward to doing it for a boss like me?

- Does my employee believe that I understand her frustrations, or do I appear mistake-proof, regret-proof … feeling-proof?

4. Valuing the employee

A team can't function at its best unless it feels valuable. That feeling can come only from you, as coach, as you provide encouragement and opportunities for increased individual success. If individuals on your team slowly get the feeling that the results of their efforts are somehow more important than *they* are, success will plummet. On the other hand, if you are each person's biggest fan … each person's most ardent supporter … you'll see results you never would have dreamed of expecting.

For example, never let a completed task go by without finding something affirming to say to the individual(s) who performed

A team can't function at its best unless it feels valuable.

it. Even if the job turned out badly, there is something positive that a truly supportive coach can find if she looks hard enough. Make it a rule, therefore, to find something about the completed job that does at least one of the following:

- **Reflects a unique attribute of the employee(s) who performed the task**

  (Bob, I could see your special eye for detail in the presentation materials!)

  — or —

- **Verifies your feeling that the employee(s) would be right for the project**

  (Kim, I knew I could count on you to meet or beat the deadline, and you were two days early!)

  — or —

- **Makes the team even better than before**

  (Thanks to you, Terry, they'll know what department to bring this kind of challenge to in the future.)

5. Listening

Too many coaches believe that what they say is more important than what they *hear* — and that listening to team members is an effortless or passive aspect of the communication process. Wrong. At least half of effective communication is listening — and truly good listening requires conscious effort. Failure to understand those two key facts can cause you to misread team-member intentions, jump to incorrect conclusions and, ultimately, antagonize your people.

Effective coaches become students of listening, and the very best ones consistently practice *five principles of listening:*

- **Listen to what the speaker is saying.**

  Do you understand what was said well enough to write it down? If not, ask questions.

At least half of effective communication is listening.

- **Listen to what is *meant*.**

  Does the speaker's tone contradict the words (e.g., sarcasm) ... does she "load" the words to sell a point of view?

  > *"I think we should buy the new folder — especially if we have to meet the quotas you forecast."*

- **"Listen" to the speaker's body language.**

  You don't have to be a psychologist to benefit from the full message your team members send as they speak verbally and nonverbally. For instance:

  (1) Is her facial expression (smile) inconsistent with other nonverbal clues (clenched fists)?

  (2) Are gestures saying something that words alone cannot (e.g., tapping fingers revealing boredom, nodding head to communicate understanding, scratching head in confusion)?

  (3) Does the person's posture suggest special meaning (e.g., slumped wearily in chair ... seated fearfully on chair edge ... pacing the floor while talking)?

- **Monitor your own nonverbal messages.**

  Does your use of eye contact show genuine interest? Or do you look as if you're preparing a response while the person is still speaking? Or, equally bad, are you checking your watch during the conversation?

  Inattentive behaviors loudly declare that you aren't interested and your employee is unimportant.

- **Ask yourself, "Can team members who talk to me expect empathy ... or judgment?"**

  Never give people the feeling that you have prejudged their communications. Your respect for a team member's ideas and feelings builds up her self-esteem ... even if you ultimately disagree with the opinion being

Does your use of eye contact show genuine interest?

expressed. But, when you show disagreement even *before* she has "made a case," you risk seriously wounding egos and self-esteem.

Listening like a coach is a very critical, very necessary business. Additional reading on this subject is highly recommended (e.g., *Learn to Listen*, by Jim Dugger, National Press Publications).

6. "Pro-active" mind-set

Another key to effective coaching is to be "pro-active." An effective coach doesn't wait for things to happen. She *makes* them happen. Are you introducing new ideas ... new solutions? Or do they happen only as a reaction to problems? A pro-active coach beats problems to the punch!

Example:

Claire:
Hi, Mike, what are you looking for in here?

Coach:
Oh, hi, Claire. I was just wondering if taking this wall out would help computer designers get to the copier room more easily.

Claire:
Are they on the other side of that wall?

Coach:
Yes.

Claire:
Wow! They have to go clear through the break room to get here now.

Coach:
I know. And they use this color copier three times more than anyone on the floor.

Claire:
They will love you if you do that.

Coach:
Well, I think I'd first better check and see if the building maintenance people would love the idea. But it sure seems as if it would make sense.

Summary

Mike is looking for ways to make his staff's job easier. Although he cannot yet promise that a wall can be removed, he is thinking about how people can do their jobs better and more effectively. Notice also that Mike has not over-promised and is thinking about the ramifications of his actions. Good ideas often come with a price tag that must be measured before a manager jumps in.

7. Effective feedback

To be effective, you also need to develop strong feedback skills. Learn how to let people know when they've done a good job or when they need to alter their course. Make it a daily habit to encourage your people ... to assure them that they are the focus of your professional life ... by regular feedback. Like listening skills, feedback demands practice, practice, practice until giving it becomes second nature.

Following are a few opportunities for feedback and some suggested methods for giving it. You will undoubtedly be able to build on this list.

Make it a daily habit to encourage your people.

61

OPPORTUNITIES FOR FEEDBACK	FEEDBACK METHOD
Successful project completion	Team meeting praising the group and acknowledging special individual effort
	Congratulatory note to all involved
Individual accomplishment	One-on-one meeting commending performance
	Letter to upper management acknowledging the individual's performance (with copy to employee)
Project in progress	Meet to review and report on progress • Analyze problems so far • Anticipate upcoming challenges • Praise achievement (individual and group)
Rumor concerning organizational or project change	Meeting or memo acknowledging the rumor, either confirming or refuting the rumor point by point
Project failure	Team or individual meeting 1. Analyze what went wrong 2. Discuss what was learned 3. Decide what to do differently next time 4. Reaffirm coach's faith in team and individual ability 5. Spotlight individual accomplishments (if any)

8. Enthusiasm and optimism

Enthusiasm and a positive outlook are communicated to a
team primarily through the manager's choice of language.
What does that mean? When you ask most people, "How are
you doing? How was lunch?" they say, "Fine." Or if you ask,
"How's it going today?", they respond, "OK." "Didn't you enjoy
that movie?" "Yeah, it was fine."

Common language responses communicate apathy, lethargy
and lack of interest. They don't get anyone anywhere.
Managers must go beyond routine responses to get better
results. So change your language. Use words like
"outstanding," "wonderful," "excellent," "great," "fantastic,"
"terrific." Start using words that go beyond the norm and
watch what happens. You'll have a different attitude toward
the commonplace.

*Use words like
"outstanding,"
"wonderful,"
"excellent," "great,"
"fantastic,"
"terrific."*

And your team members? Slowly but surely you will watch
their expressions, postures and attitudes change when you
enter the room. Their backs will straighten, the corners of their
mouths will turn up, they will unconsciously reflect your
positive spirit, in spite of themselves. But here's the best news:
Managers who have tested upbeat language in the workplace
report that after a while *just entering the office or building will
produce positive staff response.*

So when someone walks up to you and says, "How are you
doing today?" tell that person: "Great!" Now, don't use the
same word every day or all day long. That becomes
predictable and loses its effect. Vary your word choices.

In case you think it's wrong to say you feel great when you
don't, understand this: If you ask the nation's most successful
coaches how they are doing any day of the week, they'll tell
you "great, wonderful, terrific, excellent." Why? Because they
are choosing their attitudes. They are choosing how they feel!
If you doubt the truth of that practice, try it for one week.
You'll never be the same — and neither will your team!

9. Openness

Another key to effective coaching is to be non-proprietary. This means not holding things back from your team members to retain a power position. Certainly there are informational areas restricted to managers. Sharing those facts would be wrong. But withholding information that would make a team member better able to do her tasks ... maybe even better able to replace you at some point in the future ... is not protecting your job. It is jeopardizing it!

Example:

Phil:
You want me to present the new product design?

Coach:
I think you would be the perfect supervisor to do it. Your crew worked hardest at finding a solution, you put in more hours ...

Phil:
But Kathleen, it's your design idea. You came up with it.

Coach:
I may have put the period on the sentence, but a lot of team brainstorming made the words possible. Besides, you are better on your feet than I am.

Phil:
Even if that were true ... which it isn't ... my point is they'll think my crew came up with the idea.

Coach:
Then set them straight. Tell them our entire team did it. And tell them we are proud of the total effort that went into the discovery for the organization's sake.

When your people learn to trust you for tips and techniques that make them more valuable, your *own* value ... to them and to the company ... is compounded! Share the wealth and your wealth will grow.

Share the wealth and your wealth will grow.

10. Humor

Can your people laugh with you … even *at* you … without risking retribution? No work environment is less appealing than one that bans or discourages humor. Make humor a welcome and honored "co-worker" every day of the week. Why? Because when people can laugh, their mistakes and setbacks never become terminal.

Humor … especially when it comes from the top down … communicates a calming message that permeates the very fabric of a team. The message is: *People aren't perfect*. When you think about it, the idea of "perfect" projects being run by imperfect people *is* pretty funny … pretty impossible! In a wonderful way, humor acknowledges that we are all in the same leaky boat together, bailing out the water as fast as we can. Sure, our boat will make it from shore A to shore B — but only because we are a well-knit team. And only because we bail the "leaks" with humor!

With that in mind, when was the last time there was a surprise "over the hill" party for someone in your group? How about a "dubious achievement" award (e.g., an "I'm allergic to Mondays" poster)? Do you encourage it? Your team needs your endorsement in order to set into motion the freeing element of humor!

Edwin Whipple said, "Wherever you find humor, you find compassion close by." It won't happen without your help, so let your team know you endorse humor. It really isn't a character trait — it's an art that requires practice.

Laugh at your weaknesses and you'll never run out of things to laugh about.

65

CASE STUDY

After two years of concept development and testing ...
plus several presentations ... Charlotte Dunn obtained a
Small Business Loan to produce a line of specialty posters.
Key to getting the loan was the fact that she already
owned and operated a moderately profitable poster line
directed to the teen-age market. The *new* line was to be
targeted to adults for offices and homes.

With the loan money, Charlotte added four new people to
her eight-person staff and retained a new sales rep team to
market her products. Unlike the posters Charlotte
marketed to teens, the new adult posters had no words.
Only pictures. Some were scenic, some were abstract, but
all communicated a fine-art feel ... at poster prices. Limited
testing revealed support for Charlotte's idea.

Charlotte worked long hours side by side with her
graphics team, then with the printing crew, to produce a
quantity of her new posters in time for the spring New
York retail sales convention. When it looked as if the
posters might not be finished on time, Charlotte brought a
toy whip to work and laughingly "cracked" it throughout
the office for several days. When the deadline was met,
she presented everyone with a customized poster reading,
"(*Employee name*) didn't have to be crazy to come to work
here, but it helped!" Beneath the words was a photo of
Charlotte cracking her toy whip.

Sales at the convention were dismal. Orders in response to
direct-mail catalog sheets were no better. Telemarketing
efforts to help reps stimulate retail interest generated very
little success. Finally, three of Charlotte's long-time
employees came to her and suggested adding copy to the
new posters. They said they had always felt uneasy about
the wordless posters. They had always felt the idea was
wrong for the market, in spite of the favorable local focus-
group tests. Charlotte slept on it, but finally agreed.

During the next two weeks, she and her team ran the
entire new poster inventory through a sheet-fed press and
printed quotes, poetry and song lyrics onto every design.

Charlotte discovered that even the poster pictures on her remaining inventory of catalog sheets could be overprinted with the new copy. And, because the backs of the sheets were blank, she could imprint store addresses (along with a discount offer) ... then simply fold, stamp and mail to her market. Then Charlotte and the team members who suggested the line revisions flew to New York and presented the new posters to the sales rep team.

Sales crept steadily upward during the summer and fall, then jumped nicely during the holiday buying season. The results? Charlotte's team lost only 11 percent of projected sales on the new line. And, since the teen poster line had exceeded projections by 12 percent, the firm was 1 percent in the black!

At a special dinner party for "The 1-Percenter Gang," Charlotte announced plans to establish a "New Idea Review Committee" made up of employee-elected team members whose goal would be to develop, test and approve new product ideas — and to "keep crazy business owners from doing their own thing." Then Charlotte presented everyone with a $1,000 bonus check ... post-dated one year from that day ... explaining, "The dollars aren't there now, but in one year ... with a team like you ... it's money in the bank!"

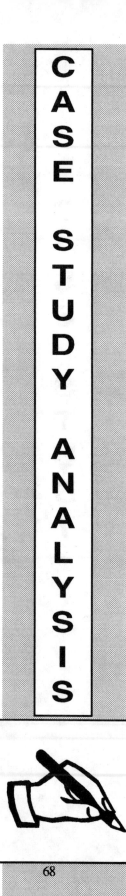

CASE STUDY ANALYSIS

1. As a StaffCoach™, what would you have done differently from Charlotte in making plans to expand?

2. What do you think Charlotte's natural StaffCoach™ style is: counselor, mentor or coach?

3. Next to each of the "*10 Tools for Building a Solid Team Foundation*," grade Charlotte from one to 10, and give a brief reason for your grade.

   - Flexibility
   - Helping
   - Empathy and understanding
   - Valuing the employee
   - Listening
   - "Pro-active" mindset
   - Effective feedback
   - Enthusiasm and optimism
   - Openness
   - Humor

4. What was the biggest thing Charlotte did right as a StaffCoach™? What was her most glaring mistake?

5. What StaffCoach™ attribute exhibited by Charlotte would be especially welcomed by your team? How could you take steps to develop that attribute?

CASE SUMMARY

A recovery plan like Charlotte's indicates the ability to learn from one's mistakes. Although this did not end in total disaster, unless something different is done in the future, this will occur again, and sales may not bounce back as strong.

One concern that appears to be left unaddressed is the lack of negative feedback from her staff. Especially in new product development, seasoned staff members must learn to speak up and discuss their concerns, not nod and see if something flies. This could have been a costly mistake.

On the positive side, the atmosphere around Charlotte's project seems positive and engaging. She truly demonstrated an awareness of the production slippage and how to get people engaged to meet the deadline. The fact that she used humor and then rewarded her team makes hard work much more palatable.

CHAPTER QUIZ

1. What is the first step in the Five-Step
    StaffCoaching™ Model?

2. What are four ways to determine an employee's
    performance level?

3. Why is knowing your StaffCoaching™ style
    important?

4. Name the ABCs of ensuring employee
    understanding.

5. List the six pitfalls to StaffCoaching™ success.

The Coaching Role

"Effective coaches focus on what they can do now to make what they want to happen in the future happen." — Jim Stanley

Imagine for a moment you coach the women's Olympic volleyball team...

You spent the entire post-season reviewing and analyzing each team member's past and potential performance level. After reviewing films, talking with each player, watching scrimmages and talking with your assistant coaches, you feel you have an idea of each player's strengths and weaknesses and the type of development program she needs to maximize her contribution to the team.

For instance, Beth has demonstrated exceptional strength and confidence in her net play over the last two years. She is a powerful and consistent point-maker in spiking situations. As coach, you need to acknowledge and clarify your expectations for Beth ... motivate her to perfect and refine her style to match the specific skills of the various teams you will face.

> *"A good coach is not necessarily a winner but a person who is a good teacher ... who doesn't abuse his or her players ... who gets the most from the players and who works within the framework of the rules."*
>
> *— Dan Devine*

Jim Stanley has more than 20 years of experience in management, training and human resource development. Jim's "real world" business experience includes nine years in the insurance industry. He was president of Success Motivation Institute and is currently Senior Associate of James K. Stanley & Associates, a management and training consulting firm. Jim holds a bachelor of science/ bachelor of administration in Accounting from Missouri Western State College and holds a master's degree in Management from Baker University.

Beth's weakness is in "team" play. She tends to be a one-woman team. Understandably, therefore, she is especially weak in "setting up" teammates to score. Beth needs you to provide mentoring in this area. So you plan to position her beside Andrea during preseason, because Andrea's ability to use the skills of her teammates has clinched many victories for you.

And Beth needs counseling. Her tendencies to criticize the play of less talented teammates and to see herself as "above" some team rules must be addressed. If they are not addressed, Beth will develop team-hindering habits that will gradually affect team morale. You decide to meet privately with Beth about these problems, explaining your concerns and establishing some short- and long-term improvement goals, with rewards and/or consequences associated with each.

Beth is only one player on your 17-member roster. The process of coaching, mentoring and counseling, therefore, is one you must go through 16 more times … it is also a process you will reevaluate and refine for each player several times during the season.

Do you know your employees this well? Do you have a sense of whether your time should be spent on coaching, mentoring or counseling? Your time and effort spent in the first phase of StaffCoaching™ assessment will pay great dividends! In this chapter we'll look at step 2, "Coaching." What is the "coaching" phase? How, when and why do you do it? These are the questions Chapter 3 is especially designed to answer.

WHAT IS THE COACHING ROLE?

To best explain your role as coach in the Five-Step StaffCoaching™ Model, let's look again at our Olympic volleyball team as an example. As coach of that team, what will you do before, during and after the game?

I. Involvement and trust

Your entire preseason will be devoted to communicating your willingness and ability to lead your team. By the time your regular season has arrived, every team member should be convinced you are the right coach for the team ... even if your decisions aren't always popular.

II. Clarify and verify

Before the game, you "clarify" expectations for your team by reviewing your game plan, and you "verify" the team's understanding by asking each team member to explain her special assignment(s) during specific game situations.

III. Affirm and acknowledge

During the game, you observe the performance of each player. You acknowledge each team member by shouting special reminders, warnings, encouragement and praise. You acknowledge the team by your visible involvement and support.

IV. Motivate and inspire

When a time-out is called just before the tie-breaking point is played, you remind each team member what is at stake ... what rewards await the winning effort you know they are capable of as individuals and as a team. You challenge them with the memory of past victories ... with the example of teams that have gone before ... with a renewed sense of all the people who are counting on their performance. Then, regardless of the game's outcome, you point to upcoming games and the victories you know your team will experience.

Those four team experiences of the volleyball coach should each be reflected in the "coaching role" of the StaffCoach™. The experiences are very similar. But while the example of a volleyball coach might be conceptually helpful, exactly how is it reflected in the organizational or corporate arena? Let's examine that now.

What will you do before, during and after the game?

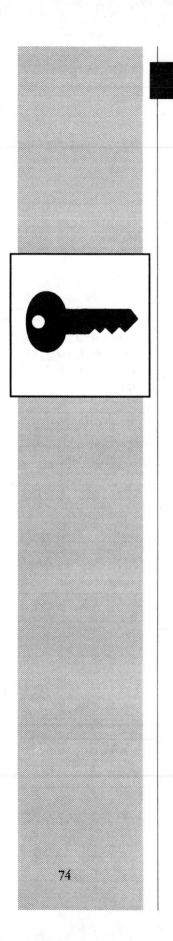

I. THE COACH'S ROLE IN COMMUNICATING INVOLVEMENT AND ESTABLISHING TRUST

Critical to your ability to function effectively in the coaching role are your willingness and ability to:

- **Become involved with your team**

- **Develop trust**

While the two work very closely together, there are differences.

1. Your involvement as a coach

In Chapter 1 ("The 10 Values of a Successful StaffCoach™"), we learned that the coach's involvement in team activities is perceived by team members as "caring." Management expert Tom Peters came up with a concept called "MBWA": *Management by Walking Around*. That means simply being *with* the members of your team. It means getting out from behind your desk ... being available ... asking questions about people and projects. How are your people doing? Can you help? Is there something you can do to improve a process?

The more you get involved with your team members, the more they will feel involved with *your* goals ... the goals of the organization. When you choose to get involved with team members, you're saying you care. You're saying each member is valuable to you and to the organization.

Think for a moment about the bosses who have made the greatest impact on your life. There are undoubtedly positive things you can say about each memorable boss. For instance, you might be able to say that he:

- **was the one who taught me the value of _____.**

- **encouraged me the most by _____.**

- **consistently exhibited the admirable quality of _____.**

There may be negative remarks you could make about the same bosses. But the good outweighed the bad, right? Additionally, there was probably one other statement you could make about that boss, a statement that makes all the others meaningful. That statement is this:

"(Boss's name) cared about who I was, what I thought and what I aspired to."

Doesn't sound like much, does it? But you know it means a lot — and so will your people!

Once you start getting involved with the people who work with you, you'll find that the next step to filling the coaching role comes very naturally.

2. Developing trust

Developing trust among team members ... and between the coach and each individual ... is one of the most important (and most overlooked) elements in any "winning season." Without trust, a team may win occasionally, but when the pressure is on ... when performance really counts ... victories without trust become less the rule and more the exception. Trust is built by laying critical foundation stones:

> *Trust is built by laying critical foundation stones.*

• *Confidentiality*
As we discussed briefly in Chapter 1, page 15, the moment you repeat something told to you in confidence, you risk the loss of mutual trust — and you may never regain it.

To illustrate this point for yourself, complete the short exercise that follows, answering candidly in light of the information provided.

You are in a private meeting with your brand new boss, briefing him on the status of the work group you supervise. You are the third of four supervisors he has met with today. During the course of your conversation, he comments to you that (1) He probably wouldn't have taken this job if the salary wasn't "top dollar" and (2) The supervisor he met with just before you apparently "has a problem at home that occupies too much of his thinking."

In response to the questions, check the boxes true or false.

I would not hesitate to tell this new boss
my personal problems.

T ☐   F ☐

I believe my new boss is fully committed
to company goals and employee development.

T ☐   F ☐

I can be completely confident that my
new boss does not talk about me
behind my back.

T ☐   F ☐

Just because my boss gossiped a little
doesn't mean I can't trust him in other areas.

T ☐   F ☐

When the job gets long and the task hard,
I know the uncompromising character
of my boss will provide needed inspiration.

T ☐   F ☐

Did you answer all five "false"? Sure. That's because the word "false" always becomes associated (consciously or subconsciously) with betrayals of confidence ... especially at the coach level! *If you learn only one lesson from this manual, learn to fight the urge to look important by telling all you know! That one truth alone is worth a whole library of books like this one.*

• *Supporting your team members*
Get in your team's corner. Let them know that, right or wrong, you rise or fall with them. If every member believes you will support him in the daily performance of team duties, your team's responsiveness to your goals will amaze you!

• *Rewarding performance*

Rewards come in all shapes and sizes. They don't have to be monetary. For instance, praise can be one of the most important of all rewards when properly used. Here are five keys to making use of a praise "bonus" for good performance.

(a) Praise only when it is truly deserved, not to pump up an employee. Overpraising has a ring of insincerity that fools no one.

(b) Criticize in private, compliment in public. When employees make mistakes, they should never be admonished publicly. However, there is much to be gained by giving public recognition.

(c) Don't be reluctant to praise people for fear of embarrassing them. Yes, be sensitive to their personalities and choose the time and place with that in mind. But people remember the honor you give them more than moments of embarrassment.

(d) Don't praise one individual or group in hopes of boosting performance in another. This kind of manipulation is easily spotted and resented!

(e) Don't wait for major accomplishments to offer praise. Rewarding small achievements with praise often plants the seed for the large achievements.

Remember, rewards can be as small as a smile or a literal pat on the back, but where rewards are given swiftly and eagerly, performance is equally swift ... equally eager!

• *Honesty*

Humorist Kin Hubbard said, "Honesty pays, but it don't seem to pay enough to suit some people." Make sure it pays enough to suit you as a coach — because nothing is more evident to team members than lack of honesty at the management level. You can't hide dishonesty, even when it is "in the best interest" of employees.

> *Rewards come in all shapes and sizes.*

> *You can't hide dishonesty.*

Example:

Mike Riley's production team is divided into three highly competitive shifts, each working the same assembly line process. About two months ago, Mike kicked off a contest that is one day away from completion. The three teams are neck and neck in a competition for output-per-hour leadership — the winning team to be the guest of the other two teams at a huge barbecue dinner and dance.

About an hour ago, Mike was told that the automotive part his teams have been so earnestly competing to produce was discontinued six days ago.

Mike's choices are:

(a) Allow the contest to continue. Don't disappoint team members by telling them they have been working all this time on a discontinued part. Wait until after the barbecue awards dinner.

(b) Allow the contest to continue. Don't tell team members at all. If anyone finds out, tell the truth: You didn't want to disappoint them.

(c) Halt the contest. Announce the part discontinuance. Tally the results of the contest so far and declare a winner based on output to date.

At this point, you may be saying, "Hey, what difference does it make? It wasn't Mike's fault. This can't be a big deal one way or the other." Can't it? Think about it.

In this instance, team morale is definitely at stake. Nearly two months of work gone up in smoke? Wow. Additionally, if competition is very close, calling the contest one day early could penalize a team that believes it has a full day to "catch up."

Further, the unfortunate fact is that the bearer of bad news is often seen in a negative light, right? It's human nature. Blameless or not, Mike isn't going to be greeted with smiles at his announcement. In fact, for the next several months he will probably be hearing, "Are you sure?" every time he assigns a new production schedule.

There's no way around it. The critical issue here is honesty. Can your team count on you to "bite the bullet" and level with them at all costs? Or are they always going to wonder if you are withholding some information on every project in order to spare their feelings? Make no mistake about it. Taking the "easy way out" of this scenario would certainly come back to haunt Mike Riley … and you!

Tell your people the truth, even if it hurts. They will learn they can depend on you to shoot straight with them — and they will reciprocate.

• Encourage communication freedom

You've heard the expression, "My door is always open." Even if that isn't the *literal* truth in your office situation, your team should be absolutely convinced that it is the *figurative* truth. When your team can trust you with any news … personal or professional … and expect you to hear them with objectivity, understanding and compassion, you are a coach who will be able to count on the "extra mile" from your people.

How do you know if you are providing communication freedom?

Free up your team by asking yourself these 10 questions:

(a) Do my people feel free to disagree with me when we talk?

(b) Is every team member aware of the basic problems I have to cope with in coaching him?

(c) Do I have difficulty telling any team member when he misses the mark — without putting him down?

(d) Does each of my people know at least two specific things he can do to get a better rating at the next performance review?

> **Tell your people the truth, even if it hurts.**

(e) Do my team members know I understand their personal goals?

(f) Are my people aware of the major decisions I have made this year in coaching them?

(g) Do I coach my people toward improvement when they need it?

(h) Does each team member understand exactly what I expect of him?

(i) Do I acknowledge the good things each of my people accomplishes?

(j) Can my people ask for help any time without feeling embarrassed?

If you can answer "yes" to at least eight of these 10 questions, then you are well on the way to measurable StaffCoach™ success!

• Consistency

If you are a leader who tends to be impulsive, or if you have high highs and low lows, heed this word of warning: Your inconsistencies can make your people paranoid.

Example:

Margaret has a long-standing department rule: Plans to take vacation days in conjunction with major holidays must be submitted to the office manager at least 90 days in advance.

With Christmas only three weeks away, her most productive tele-sales agent notified Margaret that he wanted to take four vacation days the week after Christmas to be with his fiancée in California. After much inner turmoil, Margaret reluctantly agreed.

Two days later, Margaret's least productive tele-sales agent approached her with a similar request. Margaret told her about the department rule.

Your inconsistencies can make your people paranoid.

"But you let Jim go," the employee pointed out quickly. "And I've been here longer than he has."

What should Margaret have done?

It's more a question of what she *shouldn't* have done. If a reasonable rule is established for good, profit-related reasons, it should be adhered to, barring unforeseen family emergencies, etc.

Naturally, if the rule *isn't* reasonable, it should be abolished. In this case, Margaret allowed a rule to be broken because the rule-breaker was a recognized good performer. But do you see the can of worms she has opened? The message she is communicating to her team is: "Rules are rules until I say they aren't." That will be a hard message for Margaret to live down.

Sit down and think through your decisions. If necessary, involve another manager you admire in order to make sure that you are thinking logically and that you can follow through on future policies related to the decision. Inconsistencies can be sidestepped with a little upfront patience and planning — but, once committed, they are extremely difficult to overcome.

II. THE COACH'S ROLE IN CLARIFYING EXPECTATIONS AND VERIFYING UNDERSTANDING

Having the finest game plan for the best team does not guarantee success unless that plan is communicated and understood. That's why coaches of professional athletes spend so much time reviewing and discussing game films, designing play books, conducting "chalk talks," diagraming sideline plays, etc. Many coaches believe that the game is won or lost before the actual competition, depending on how well the game plan has been presented and understood by team members.

Whether or not that is always the case in sports could be debated. But there is no question that victories in the

> *Many coaches believe that the game is won or lost before the actual competition.*

organizational environment cannot happen without clear, purposeful direction from the StaffCoach™ and consistent team-member comprehension. Sure, a team can fail despite having those key elements, through factors beyond its control (e.g., policy changes, equipment or material alterations, inadequate or incorrect information). But it can't win without the key elements!

With that in mind, let's look at ways you can ensure consistent clarity on the giving as well as the receiving end of coach-generated communications.

1. **Clarifying Your Expectations as Coach: How to Say What You Think You Said**

   • *Communicate in terms team members can understand.*

   Have you ever been in a meeting and listened to a well-meaning, intelligent professional talk gibberish? Everyone has. "Gibberish" is trade talk or industry jargon — words and expressions that mean something to some specialized group somewhere but are meaningless to the general public. Hearing gibberish is a maddening experience, particularly when you really want to know and act on the information being communicated (or rather, *not* being communicated).

   You have three choices in those instances:

   (a) Smile and nod and hope no one asks you to repeat what you've heard.

   (b) Risk looking dumb by saying, "What does that word mean?"

   (c) Hope someone else will look dumb and ask the questions for you.

   A StaffCoach™ can't afford to put his team members in that position, especially when communicating instructions, action plans or goals.

Hearing gibberish is a maddening experience.

Example:

Coach (on phone):
Bernie, would you go to my office and bring a couple of things down to this meeting for me?

Bernie:
Sure, Ray, what things?

Coach:
Well, there were some year-end budget materials I've been working with. They are stacked on the far right-hand corner of my desk.

Bernie:
I think I see the pile from here.

Coach:
Good. What I need immediately from that stack are two files: the Income Statement and the Balance Sheet. The rest can wait. But everyone is waiting for those things down here.

Bernie:
No problem. Except, um ...

Coach:
Yeah?

Bernie:
What do those things you just said *look* like, exactly?

Everybody knows what an income statement and balance sheet look like, right? Wrong. It's always a dangerous assumption to think that your team members share your experience or understand any concept critical to carrying out instructions.

• *Avoid using abbreviations or nicknames even when "everyone" knows what they mean.*

> *"Everybody plan on having your IRC on the TL dock ... clean and ready for old 'Iron Shoulders' tomorrow morning at the latest."*

Sound like an exaggeration? No, it's for real. Every organization, yours included, has pet abbreviations that save time and effort. However, for the benefit of anyone who may have forgotten, who may be new or who may confuse one abbreviation with the other, the clearest instructions are always abbreviation-free!

• *Don't permit sight or sound competition.*

Anyone who has ever stood on the fringes of a crowd and strained to hear a speaker above traffic noise, laughter, applause, etc., understands the importance of this rule. If your listeners must resort to asking a nearby co-worker, "What did she say?" or "When did he say it's due?", you're asking for trouble. Pick a communication environment that is distraction-free ... that will comfortably accommodate your audience and permit every attendee a full view of the speaker.

If you think the acoustics warrant it, use a microphone and amplifier. Even when your meeting involves only a few people, avoid environments that allow external noise, passersby or phone interruptions to distract your team.

• *Improve clarity by using illustrations and examples.*

Understanding is doubled or tripled when it is made "concrete." That's just the way the human mind works.

Example:

Coach:
OK now, remember, these trucks will be overloaded if the shingles are stacked higher than (pause) ... let's see ... (looks around) ... Hank, how tall are you?

The clearest instructions are always abbreviation-free!

Understanding is doubled or tripled when it is made "concrete."

Hank:
Oh, about 5' 11" I think.

Coach:
Perfect! Stack the shingles no higher than Hank, and we'll be fine.

Occasionally, using a projector or flip chart to help team members visualize the plan can be helpful.

Coach:
OK, this is a bird's-eye view of the stage. Everyone understand what you're looking at? (general murmur of assent). OK, then. Betsy, when the lights come up, you walk on the stage from Position "A," here, and move to Position "B," the podium, where Cliff will have the projector controls waiting for you. Got it?

Betsy:
Is Position "A" where the stairs are?

Coach:
Right. Now, Wes, when Betsy stops at the podium, you turn your spotlight on Position "C," over here, and hold it for the count of ...

The point is, every direction you pass on to team members can be clarified by communications *tailored to the situation.*

• ***Additional communication methods might include:***

Role-playing:
Explain by acting out a desired activity.

Outcome-contrast:
Describe what not to do, usually based on past team experience.

> *You have two chances of building a strong team without communication: slim and none.*

85

Coach:
So, when we finally get this display ready to ship, it should look like … well … Ann, remember that job we shipped for Puritan?

Ann:
Do I ever! (laughter)

Coach:
Well, it shouldn't look like that!

Team-member experts:
The team can sometimes "hear" most clearly from a veteran in their own ranks, someone they respect and who has proven to be proficient at the task that needs describing. Just make sure you and the "vet" have time to review what he plans to communicate.

There are as many ways to clarify instructions and goals through examples and illustrations as there are coaches. So don't be afraid to be creative in your efforts to provide your team with memorable, meaningful communications!

• *Organize before communicating*

In the rush of busy days, when the procedures seem obvious and the projects seem predictable, failure to organize before communicating important directions or goals is very tempting … very common. In spite of that, remember: Organized effort never results from disorganized input! The responsibility for project progress … for tasks that move from start to finish smoothly, on time and without hitches … rests squarely on the coach and his ability to outline organized activity.

Never shortcut the organizational phase of your team communications. Two ways to avoid that are:

(1) Write down your instructions or information

Directions the team must act on are three to four times more likely to be followed correctly when written! Why?

Each new day presents a manager with first-rate opportunities to avoid second-rate options.

For at least three reasons:

(a) Team members can reread and make notes on the facts you provide in writing.

(b) Misunderstandings or inaccuracies regarding names or numbers are avoided.

(c) Responsibilities and expectations are documented in advance.

It may take more time and effort to put your team communications in writing, but the effort will pay off in fewer errors, less time policing performance, and consistency in follow-through.

(2) What, Who, Why, How, Where, When, What

Whatever form your communication takes ... memo, one-on-one, team presentation, conference call, etc. ... a formula many coaches have found consistently effective in communicating informational essentials is the "3-1-3" Method. The numbers stand for three "W"s, one "H" and three "W"s (What, Who, Why, How, Where, When, What). While the order may vary, these letters represent the information elements most of your directions should include:

WHAT	Explain the project or goal
WHO	Assign responsibility for follow-through
WHY	The reasons for and benefits of the task
HOW	What action will achieve the goal
WHERE	Relevant project locations (conference rooms, warehouses, client offices, departments, etc.)
WHEN	The project timetable; start and finish dates
WHAT	The consequences of success or failure; rewards and penalties

The "3-1-3" Method

Here is a memo that makes obvious use of the "3-1-3" formula:

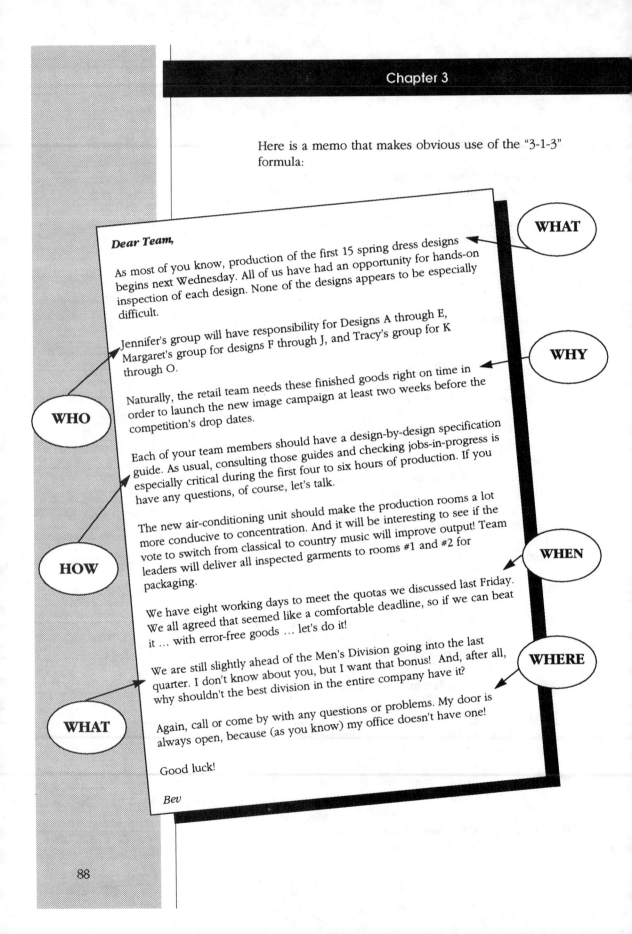

WHAT

WHY

WHO

HOW

WHEN

WHERE

WHAT

Dear Team,

As most of you know, production of the first 15 spring dress designs begins next Wednesday. All of us have had an opportunity for hands-on inspection of each design. None of the designs appears to be especially difficult.

Jennifer's group will have responsibility for Designs A through E, Margaret's group for designs F through J, and Tracy's group for K through O.

Naturally, the retail team needs these finished goods right on time in order to launch the new image campaign at least two weeks before the competition's drop dates.

Each of your team members should have a design-by-design specification guide. As usual, consulting those guides and checking jobs-in-progress is especially critical during the first four to six hours of production. If you have any questions, of course, let's talk.

The new air-conditioning unit should make the production rooms a lot more conducive to concentration. And it will be interesting to see if the vote to switch from classical to country music will improve output! Team leaders will deliver all inspected garments to rooms #1 and #2 for packaging.

We have eight working days to meet the quotas we discussed last Friday. We all agreed that seemed like a comfortable deadline, so if we can beat it ... with error-free goods ... let's do it!

We are still slightly ahead of the Men's Division going into the last quarter. I don't know about you, but I want that bonus! And, after all, why shouldn't the best division in the entire company have it?

Again, call or come by with any questions or problems. My door is always open, because (as you know) my office doesn't have one!

Good luck!

Bev

As mentioned, the order of your "W"s will vary with your situation, but the simplicity of this formula and its "catch all" power will prove to be one of your key communication allies.

2. Verifying Team Understanding: How to Hear What They Think They Heard

• *Ask questions*

Hopefully, by now you have established the kind of open, non-threatening work environment that encourages every team member to ask any question any time. The old adage, "The only dumb questions are the ones never asked," is still true and very important to the ongoing growth and development of any team. Even when you are sure this freedom exists, however, the way you ask verifying questions can reveal questions your team members didn't know they had.

"Is there anything that might still be a little unclear about what I've said?"

This question, or one like it, can encourage team members to search their understanding and verbalize any doubts that may exist ... especially when the coach asks it in an agreeable ... even expectant ... tone of voice. Simply barking the words "Any questions?" (particularly in a group environment) is deadly. You might as well add, "Or are you too dumb to understand the *first* time?"

Other kinds of question-phrasing some managers have found conducive to employee responses are:

"This is pretty complicated stuff, so don't hesitate to tell me when I can make something clearer."

"I expect lots of questions about this, so just stop me when you have one."

"Let's stop now and deal with questions you have about all this. I had lots myself when I first heard it."

> **The only dumb questions are the ones never asked.**

Do you sense the advance acceptance in these questions? Wouldn't you have been grateful to have heard questions like them in meetings when you wanted to clarify something but were too intimidated to ask? Your team members will be just as grateful!

These three questions communicate very encouraging messages: As coach, I'm not always as clear as I want to be ... I feel your questions are justified ... I've had questions like you may have right now.

You may discover your own ways of probing for uncertainties that are just as encouraging ... and even better. Remember: Unanswered questions are like bad checks. They will return to demand your attention ... with penalties!

- *Hypothetical scenarios*

Another helpful technique for flushing out misconceptions of information you communicate is to pose hypothetical situations based on the project and procedures you have outlined.

Example:

Coach:
OK, now, just to make us all feel more comfortable with what we're about to do, let's make a few assumptions. Ben, what happens if we get a few days into this project and we get bad material on one of the lines, like we did on the Acme job last year?

Ben:
I notify Pat and switch over to one of the other products until she gets back to me.

Coach:
And what do you do, Pat?

Pat:
I update you and alert at least two of the backlog supervisors to prepare for line substitutions in case materials can't be found. Then I call Bill for a material trace.

Coach:
Exactly!

Ben:
Shouldn't I update you also, Bill, in case I can't get Pat
right away?

Coach:
You know, that's probably a good idea, Ben. That
would cover all the bases even earlier. Good thinking!

Hypothetical scenarios can be fun and enlightening,
depending on the situation. A word of caution, however:
Such scenarios can also sound childish or insulting to
highly professional mentalities. You must make that call.
In any case, scenario development is nearly always best in
a group setting where individuals can interact and not feel
as if they are being graded by their responses or put on
the "hot seat."

• Reports on progress

A popular method of verifying team understanding of your
directions is written or verbal project progress reports.
These can be as simple and informal as daily or weekly
coffee meetings casually discussing job flow. Or they can
be as regimented as submitting forms at specific project
points or job phases. In either case, team-member reports
might use the kind of outline that follows on the next
page.

*Scenarios tend to
work best in a
group setting.*

Reports on Progress

WHERE WE'VE BEEN:

The successes _____

The problems/setbacks _____

Questions and solutions _____

WHERE WE ARE:

The successes _____

The problems/setbacks _____

Questions and solutions _____

WHERE WE'RE GOING:

The successes _____

The problems/setbacks _____

Questions and solutions _____

> *"Genius begins great works; labor finishes them."*
>
> *—Joubert*

Whether written or oral, reports should update the coach on what is going right, what isn't, what might not go right and what uncertainties or problem-solving tactics the team is involved with.

Your report outline (if you choose to use one) may be quite different from this one, but a standardized structure for reporting progress can assure everyone that nothing is falling through the cracks.

• *Listen to the feedback your verification efforts generate*

You may remember that the subtitle of this section is "How to Hear What They Think They Heard" (page 89). You can't do that without listening. In Chapter 2 (pages 58-60), we focused on some of the techniques important in hearing "the message behind the message." The tone of a team member's response to your questions, as well as facial expressions, gestures and postures can send signals that verify or contradict his oral message.

Example:

Coach:
Well, Leslie, I guess that's about it. Are you clear on everything ... any questions at all?

Leslie (furrowed brow):
Not a thing.

Coach:
Uh-huh. It's a lot to take in on such short notice. You're not even a little unclear on something?

Leslie (eyes downcast, arms folded):
It's all *perfectly* clear.

Coach:
I guess I'm sensing there may be something troubling you about this project that I may be making hard for you to share. I think it's important that we open up to each other at this stage, Leslie.

Leslie (chin lifted, eye contact from down nose, tone of resentment):
It's nothing, really. I'll admit I did think our team was ready for something a little more challenging.

Coach:
That's perfectly true. That's why yours is the only team that will be doing two projects this week — this one and the Kmart job we are expecting Thursday.

Leslie (brightening, straightening in chair):
Oh! The Kmart job?

Coach:
Right. I was going to tell you about that once we had the specifics of this project worked out.

Leslie (solid eye contact, leaning forward eagerly):
Well, this one is clear, Gale. I've got a good handle on it. So if you want to talk about the Kmart project, I'm ready.

> *Ideas work best when YOU do.*

Look back at just the spoken responses of Leslie before Gale told her about the Kmart job. They are positive, but her expression, tone and posture are negative.

Obviously, in an actual situation, your job will be much tougher. You'll have no written dialogue descriptions to compare and contrast. But being sensitive to responses and hearing more than words as you attempt to verify understanding will be of ongoing importance.

Probe for the reasons behind contradictory messages. They signal underlying problems that could sabotage communication and project success.

III. THE COACH'S ROLE IN AFFIRMING THE TEAM

Once you have established a trusting coach/team relationship … one in which the lines of two-way communication function without interference, you are ready to turn your attention to another critical area of coach/team interactivity — that of affirming team members in their efforts to improve performance.

> *No team member works well for long without a compliment.*

Like rewarding employees, affirming or complimenting them on efforts and attitude must become second nature to the winning coach. No team member works well for long without a compliment — and no coach compliments people if his view of an employee is always negative.

That's why this process must start with the coach. A positive or negative attitude is a choice the coach makes every day he goes to work. "Pretty extreme statement," you might be thinking. Nevertheless, it's true. Consciously or unconsciously you choose how you will respond to the people and events of every single day.

For instance, if your first thoughts about the office as you turn on the shower or lay out the clothes you plan to wear are anxious, agitated or fearful, you will make a conscious or unconscious decision to do one of two things: Keep thinking those negative thoughts, or think of the things you look forward to about your day.

1. Keep thinking those negative thoughts...

...turning them over and over in your mind — usually looking for some way to avoid or defuse the situation you are dreading. It's a little like "chewing day-old gum." Worrying ceased producing any benefit long ago, but your jaws keep right on moving out of habit.

What happens when you choose to allow this thought process? Everything is colored by the negative lens through which your mind views the day. The drive to work is chaos. It seems that all you encounter at work is bad news. Even the good news isn't as good as it could be. Unless something happens to jar you out of this negative mindset (e.g., you win the Publisher's Clearinghouse Sweepstakes), your day will end no better than it started — and the next morning it will pick up where it left off!

Ninety-nine percent of the time this process is totally unconscious. After all, who would *want* that kind of day otherwise? People allow it because they aren't aware that the choice to start or stop it is almost entirely up to them! Now let's look at another option.

2. Think of the things you look forward to about your day.

Unlike the *un*pleasant prospects your day might hold, focusing on the positives will rarely happen unconsciously — not at first. It must be a conscious choice. One good way to do that is to make a list of all the things you like about your work. If you are like most professionals, the good things about your job outweigh the bad by at least 75 percent to 25 percent. The challenge, therefore, is focus — choosing to see the 75 percent rather than the 25 percent. How? Sit down and list your job pluses. The big things and the small things (your office is close to home, cafeteria food is great, you get a paid vacation, etc.).

Now, every day for two weeks, read that list from start to finish before you do anything in the morning. No coffee, no shower, no anything ... not until you read that list all the way through. The results? Watch and see. Your tendency to focus on the "dreaded" aspects of the day will gradually lessen. In

> *Worry is interest paid on trouble before it is due.*

spite of yourself, you'll find yourself thinking, "Yes, but remember the list of good things ... ." And you'll discover a new tendency to spot the good side of situations in every area of your day. If you doubt it, try it. A lot of people who thought it couldn't possibly work are recommending it to others today!

3. List the job strengths and positive character traits of one team member each day.

Let's start this exercise with a "problem" employee in your area. Now, write down four compliments you might honestly give that employee if you really tried. It may be a little difficult. Our brains tend to focus on negative memories rather than on the potential for new tomorrows. If you were told to write down four reasons why that same person is a problem employee, it would probably be much easier.

To get you started, a sample "Team Booster" form has been filled out for a hypothetical employee — and a blank form is included to copy for your own use.

> *"Most folks are about as happy as they make up their minds to be."*
>
> *— Abraham Lincoln*

Team Booster Forms:

Team Member___*Robert*_____

ATTRIBUTE	***COMPLIMENT***	***DATE DONE***
Never misses work.	If everyone had your attendance record, we'd probably always be ahead of schedule.	Mon. 2/4
Quiet. Doesn't disturb others by talking loudly.	We all need to help each other concentrate on the job by keeping our voices down ... like Robert.	
Desk is always neat.	It's nice to know there's an orderly desk I can show when visiting clients drop in.	
Doesn't take long lunches.	Thanks for being trustworthy about lunch hours.	

Team Member_____

ATTRIBUTE	***COMPLIMENT***	***DATE DONE***

You'll notice that none of these positive attributes is exceptionally noteworthy. There are no mentions of job achievements or professional skills. Many of the qualities you find to compliment in your own team members may fall into similar categories. But track the process for a few months and you'll begin to find new positive things to say as your team responds to your affirmation!

Naturally, compliments should not be given so frequently that they appear forced or phony. But be regular. Your team needs it — and *you* need it!

Finally, once you have identified compliments that will affirm even your most difficult team member, decide *when* to make the compliments. Be specific. Mark your calendar to remind yourself to praise him. You'll be creating success patterns by recognizing and rewarding team achievements.

As a coach, you must train yourself to find the positive in any dilemma ... any challenge ... any personnel situation. Your ability to see "small victories" in circumstances that look like disasters to others will make you and your team members less inclined to expect and accept defeat.

IV. THE COACH'S ROLE IN MOTIVATING AND INSPIRING

Finally, your job as coach means helping your team catch a vision for victory in every task. It means energizing your people from the outside until they gradually begin energizing themselves from the inside. No, you don't have to be a cheerleader. You just have to be willing to be involved with your people, to earn their trust by being real and by respecting their points of view, to keep the lines of communication clear, and to affirm their efforts to be the best they can be.

In short, *motivation and inspiration are the logical outgrowths of everything you have read in this chapter up to this point.* Logical, but not automatic. As coach, you still provide the vision. You still provide the challenge to look beyond the tasks at hand to new horizons.

You don't have to be a cheerleader.

For instance, you probably already know that money is not the *only* performance motivator. Sometimes it isn't even the *best* one. Not that it should be downgraded: It is certainly as valuable as most motivators, but it isn't a *substitute* for them. Every serious study of team behavior over the last 30 years shows that numerous short-term and long-term career incentives are more important than "income increases" when it comes to energizing employee performance, morale and loyalty.

Based on those studies, the following exercise is designed to help you find motivators of special relevance to your own people. Remember — think of answers you believe would be especially significant as motivators in your own special team environment.

Exercise:

1. Shared goals

In the blanks on the left, list three goals you and the people on your team would consider desirable ... unanimously. Product quality might be a common goal. Manageable deadlines might be another. What others would be uniquely true for you and the people on your team?

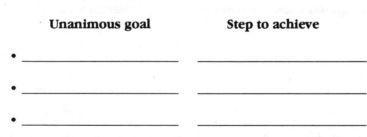

    Unanimous goal   **Step to achieve**

- _____ _____

- _____ _____

- _____ _____

In the blanks at the right, write one step that could be taken to achieve each goal.

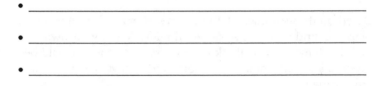

2. Self-esteem

List three ways you might increase the self-esteem of each member on your team. Be specific and realistic. Don't say, "Compliment them more often." Instead say, "Compliment Pat on her performance twice a week starting at lunch next Tuesday." In what other ways can you help maintain the self-esteem of the people on your team?

- _____

- _____

- _____

3. Good communication

In the blanks below at the left, list three ways you can improve communications between team members. Maybe a Friday afternoon "Coffee and Recap" meeting would help air any lingering problems or resentments. How about an employee-produced newsletter? Use your imagination — and solicit ideas from the entire team.

Communication improvement   **Step to achieve**

- _____   _____

- _____   _____

- _____   _____

In the blanks at the right, write one step that could be taken to achieve each goal.

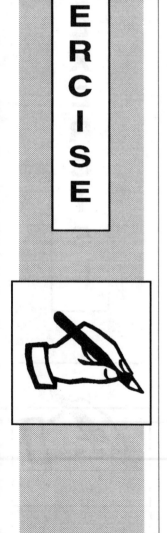

**E
X
E
R
C
I
S
E**

4. Growth opportunity

In the blanks at the left, list three ways to empower your team. Are there functions you or a supervisor perform that the team could do? Are there procedures that might be improved from *within* the team rather than imposed from outside? For instance, do you have a problem-solving committee among your team members to handle selected difficulties? Is there an idea development committee? Have you considered asking team members to write their own job descriptions? How might your team members be encouraged to take ownership in company plans and policies — and grow as individuals — through new responsibilities?

Empowerment opportunity   **Step to achieve**

• _____   _____

• _____   _____

• _____   _____

In the blanks at the right, write one step that could be taken to achieve each goal.

5. Trust and respect

On the following page, in the blanks at the left, identify three ways to build mutual trust and respect between you and your team members. Do you spend individual time with each member weekly (not just to correct them)? What could you do that would show your commitment to the team's best interests without sacrificing organizational standards or goals? Have you ever ordered in pizza and invited team members to a luncheon brainstorming session? Do you have a team picnic? Dinner? Night out at the ballgame? What could you do to demonstrate your belief that you have the best group of people any manager could ask for?

EXERCISE

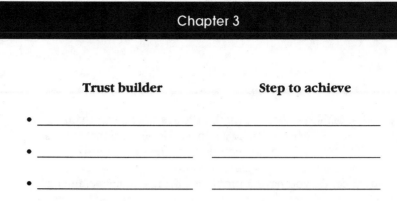

	Trust builder	Step to achieve
•	_____	_____
•	_____	_____
•	_____	_____

In the blanks at right above, write one step that could be taken to achieve each goal.

You have now compiled a list of non-money motivators that can bolster morale, improve performance and heighten commitment at least as much as a salary increase. Put them to work today!

EIGHT HURDLES TO PERFORMING YOUR COACHING ROLE

You can't be a good coach without also knowing the attitudes and actions that can sabotage the best-laid managerial plans. Certain approaches to coaching can be disastrous, as many well-intentioned managers have discovered too late.

Here are the eight most common errors in coaching that undermine the performance of any work team ... however talented it may be!

1. **Detached leadership**
2. **Lack of goals**
3. **Failure to provide perspective**
4. **Failure to be specific**
5. **Failure to secure commitment**
6. **Taking the course of least resistance**
7. **Failure to identify results**
8. **Impatience**

1. Detached leadership

Detached leaders isolate themselves from people. They seem to believe it's undignified to get too involved with team members. They tend to spend a lot of time alone in their offices. They communicate a "lonely-at-the-top" attitude — one that says it's not organizationally healthy to rub shoulders with the "common" people.

The truth is, *nothing* is more important than involvement and communication with the people with whom we work. Management expert Tom Peters summed it up this way: *"The most successful managers spend 75 percent of their time with their people."* Do you spend 75 percent of your time with members of your team? Or do you think, "How would I get my work done if I spent that much time with them?"

Consider this: If it's true that you as a coach exist to get results not from yourself but from the people who work for you, where should you be spending most of your time? Remember also that everything starts at the top. Your attitude affects the people who work for you. That's why detached leadership can be such a problem. If you show no interest in or concern for your people, why should they give your goals or your standards a place of importance in their minds and hearts?

2. Lack of goals

If you lack goals, sooner or later you'll have serious coaching problems. You'll be like a ship without a rudder — going wherever the wind and waves take you.

What are your team goals ... short-range and long-range? Have you listed some of them on page 99? Examples might include:

- Increase sales quotas by 10 by one year from today
- Schedule every team member for a WordPerfect computer class
- Turn over the budgeting process to each team supervisor
- Implement a Total Quality Service program next fall
- Bring in outside training for handling conflict and criticism at work

> *Detached leaders spend a lot of time alone in their offices.*

W I N

Can your team members list your goals? To win, every team needs to know **W**hat's **I**mportant **N**ow (W.I.N.). The key word in that formula is "Now." For instance, have you ever stared at your "things to do" list and ended up doing nothing at all? The sheer volume of work absolutely blew you away! We have all done that. But then somehow each of us learns that to get all our tasks done we simply have to tackle them one at a time. First things first. What's important *now?* Your team needs to know that. Only when you tell them the priorities will you see measurable progress.

In addition, goals you and your team settle on must be:

(a) *Consistent with organizational direction —*
In other words, no team is an island. Apart from the organizational glue that holds you together, the team really has no professional reason for being. Therefore, make certain that your team goals line up with organizational directions. Don't set goals independent of the organizational structure (e.g., a three-day work week) or you will be in for disappointments.

When goals conflict with organizational plans, people will grumble at least and possibly rebel.

Some examples of aligned organizational goals include:

- Employees can earn a "floating holiday" if they will work one day during company shut-down. This meets the organization's need for minimal business operations while giving employees a day off of their choosing at a later date.

- All team members will receive a year-end bonus of 10 percent of their salary if the team meets its goals. In this case, both employee and organization receive what they are seeking, money in the pocket.

- Each department will assume responsibility for hosting a quarterly "all-company" meeting that combines progress reports, food and fun. In this case, the "all-company" meetings offer an important collection of company employees featuring camaraderie and business reporting.

(b)   *Simple but exciting —*
In order for your team goals to excite the team, you need team-member input to and ownership of each goal. That's why some very successful StaffCoaches™ have established team committees to brainstorm goals, submit Team Mission Statements and develop a plan for measuring progress. Others have identified goals *for* their teams but then turned them over to self-directed team committees to report regularly on progress toward achieving the goals.

In any case, exciting, motivational goals must offer benefits your team views as worthy and real.

(c)   *In front of your people daily —*

Some obvious ways to keep team goals in front of members daily are:

- Progress charts (updated daily)
- Team newsletters
- Daily "pump up" coffee sessions
- Banners, buttons, posters … even bumper stickers
- T-shirts

You will undoubtedly have some spirit-lifting ideas of your own. But remember, if you aim at nothing, you can be sure that you will hit it!

> *Motivational goals must offer benefits your team views as worthy.*

EXERCISE

In the chart below, plan your next month. How can you keep team goals in front of your staff, doing different things daily, weekly, and monthly? Write what you will do in the boxes below using the ideas listed previously and some of your own.

	Monday	Tuesday	Wednesday	Thursday	Friday
Week #1					
Week #2					
Week #3					
Week #4					

Now that it's written, don't forget the most important part of this exercise: Follow it!

3. Failure to provide perspective

Ever get assigned a task that didn't make sense to you? Ever tackle a job without having the slightest idea how it fit with anything ... how it worked within the "big picture"? You may have done it ... even done it well ... but it wasn't your best effort, and it wasn't satisfying or rewarding.

People who don't know why they do what they do are people who don't give their best. That's because they don't see their job as important. When you give them the "why" of their task, they can see its relevance — and real job satisfaction can take place.

If you are like more than 65 percent of the managers in mid-size to large American organizations, people who work for you don't understand what they contribute to the overall scheme of things. You should go to those people and say, "I'm sure you understand the importance of your job, but let me tell you how important *I* think it is." Then give them the "whys" of their job and how it works within the organization. Chances are good they will take more pride and interest in what they're doing. The results? They will begin to assume "ownership" of their performance. They will gradually become self-starters ... their own vision-setters. They will have their own *internal* reasons for performing regardless of the *external* incentives offered!

4. Failure to be specific

You've seen this happen: A manager tells the team what he wants in broad terms. Then the manager waits for somebody to start doing it. What happens when you wait for self-starters? You'll wait forever. Don't wait ... motivate! Tell people ... specific people ... exactly what you expect of them.

Example:

Coach:
You're right, Tom, your sales are down. *Way* down. What do you think the problem is?

Tom:
I honestly don't know. I'm doing all the things that *used* to work ... making at least 30 calls a day ... following up with company literature, networking for referrals. It's frustrating!

Coach:
Hmm. Might be time for something new.

Tom:
Like what?

Coach:
Well, you've been pretty active in church and Scouting over the years, haven't you?

If you aim at nothing, you can be sure that you will hit it!

Don't wait ... motivate!

Tom:
Very active.

Coach:
That probably means you've come to understand the people in those settings ... what they value and what they don't. You know what gets their attention.

Tom:
If you're suggesting that I call people I know from church and Scouting, I've done some of that ever since ...

Coach:
No, I'm suggesting something more. What if you put together a letter tailored to each of those markets? A letter that speaks to their values and needs ... positioning yourself as being uniquely able to understand them and meet those needs?

Tom:
Like I can give them a level of trust they can't get from others in my business?

Coach:
Right.

Tom:
What about the company brochure?

Coach:
Well, since it hasn't set the world on fire for you lately, why not try 20 or 30 letters without it? When you get appointments from phone follow-up, you can always give it to them then.

Tom:
You think this approach might work? I'm not really the best letter writer in the world.

Coach:
Do a couple of rough drafts by Monday and we'll work on polishing it together. Sure, I think the idea has possibilities — and with you behind it, I think it has real potential!

Give your people goals, some ideas about how to accomplish them ... a vote of confidence ... and a deadline. That's when "self-starters" can really shine!

5. Failure to secure commitment

If no mutual commitment exists between the coach and the team, there isn't much of a team at all. You must have mutual commitment to goals. How do you get it? By spending time together. The more time you spend with someone, the better you can identify with his abilities and vision. You must spend time sharing goals, problems, victories and even fears. Mutual commitment develops only through time and effort. It all comes back to the "MBWA" principle mentioned at the beginning of this chapter — "Management by Walking Around."

Mutual commitment comes from spending time together.

6. Taking the course of least resistance

If you settle for what you know is less than the best you or your people can deliver, you may avoid confrontation — you may even think you're "cutting your team some slack." But the reality is that you undermine not only your coaching credibility but also your team's long-term viability. When a team faces a tough opponent ... win or lose ... it comes out better than if it had faced some "no-contest" challenge.

Example:

Coach:
Kim, I just finished reading through the copy you wrote for the Father's Day cards. Some neat stuff.

Kim:
Just "neat"? I was hoping for "splendid" or maybe even "dynamite."

Coach:
Well, it shows your talent. You couldn't hide that if you tried. But it's just not the "Kim quality" I always look forward to.

Kim:

What's wrong with it? The editor asked for 10 tries and I gave her 16!

Coach:

I noticed that. Editors always appreciate extras — but I also noticed in her requisition that she asked for some of that newer metric copy like you did during the Fall Seasons brainstorm session last month.

Kim:

That stuff takes *time*, John. Maybe if she saw what I've done she'd like it OK.

Coach:

She might. But doing that wouldn't line up with our team Mission Statement … the part that says we will "meet and exceed requisitions with the best, most original material we can create." You wrote that, as I recall?

Kim:

Ouch!

Coach:

I think a couple more of those newer approaches would be all this assignment needs to be "dynamite," to use your word. And we're still two days away from the due date.

Kim:

OK, Simon Legree. I'll do it. But you're a hard man.

Coach:

Only because you've helped me recognize excellent copywriting when I see it.

Notice how this confrontation doesn't focus as much on the project deficiency as it does on the coach's pride in and expectations of the employee? A coach always urges his team to be the best it can be — and that occasionally calls for "corrective inspiration."

Don't ever hesitate to ask your team members for their best. When they give it, they'll always be glad they did!

> **Don't ever hesitate to ask your team members for their best.**

7. Failure to identify results

The seventh block to coaching success is having no clear sense of results. If the people on your team don't feel like they're getting results, they will gradually lose motivation. When you accomplish a task or a goal, let your people know.

Many coaches have found that "Project Recaps" are helpful in ensuring this vital finishing touch in any team effort. PR's can take many forms, written or verbal. But however you choose to acknowledge team achievement, recapping a project should include at least seven points, as shown in the sample here.

When you accomplish a task, let your people know.

PROJECT RECAP

- **What was the original project goal?**

  To pave six miles of cracked interstate highway

- **What made it difficult and/or important?**

  Unseasonably hot spring weather made it hard. The approaching summer vacation traffic made it urgent.

- **Who worked on the project?**

  Three five-member crews headed by Pat, Roy and Terry

- **What made the person(s) right for the task? Be specific.**

  Their record for meeting repair deadlines is the best in the Highway Department.

- **What were the good aspects of the project? Pinpoint individual effort.**

  Roy's jackhammer team worked overtime four days in a row. Terry's grader driver discovered a good new technique for preventing crumbling shoulders.

- **What problems called for solutions-in-progress?**

  Pat's crew had to pump concrete at night to fill three eroded or collapsed sections.

- **What aspects of this project make you as coach proud of the team?**

  It was the fastest time ever recorded for paving so much highway.

This example could be used by the coach as his speaking outline in a group meeting or as an outline for a memo to each team member. In any case, Project Recaps are simple but powerful team motivators. Why? Because it's vitally important for team members to see results. There are few things as satisfying as being able to say, "We did that! I had a part in making it happen!"

PROJECT RECAP

1. **What was the original project goal?**

2. **What made it difficult and/or important?**

3. **Who worked on the project?**

4. **What made the person(s) right for the task? Be specific.**

5. **What were the good aspects of the project? Pinpoint individual effort.**

6. **What problems called for solutions-in-progress?**

7. **What aspects of this project make you as coach proud of the team?**

8. Impatience

To succeed as a coach, you must develop patience. When you have explained something to someone 10 times and the person asks you to repeat it just one more time, you must learn to smile and repeat it once again. When your team suffers setbacks or doesn't reach goals as quickly as you would like, you must learn to smile, help your people pick themselves up and go at it again. You must learn to tell your team members over and over that you believe in them ... that you know they can do it. Why? Because then they will gradually begin to have patience with themselves!

The way that works is not at all complicated. The fact is, people fail. When they do, they will either (1) lose patience with themselves and quit or pout or both — or they will (2) understand that failure doesn't diminish them in your eyes and try again!

As you model patience for your team, they will begin to understand that your patience is more than a comforting character attribute. It's a response to *reality* — a response to your team's humanity. That growing, subconscious awareness will set your team free to try anything once — but, more importantly, to try anything *again!*

Exercise:

In the spaces provided under the eight hindrances to coaching beginning on the next page, write what you think are the opposite, *positive* qualities of each hindrance (e.g., the opposite of "Detached leadership" might be "Involved leadership") — then briefly describe how each positive quality could be applied right now in your own team environment.

EXERCISE

113

1. Detached leadership

The opposite of this might be _____

How would my team benefit immediately if I applied this coaching quality?

_____

_____

_____

2. Lack of goals

The opposite of this might be _____

How would my team benefit immediately if I applied this coaching quality?

_____

_____

_____

3. Failure to provide perspective

The opposite of this might be _____

How would my team benefit immediately if I applied this coaching quality?

_____

_____

_____

4. Failure to be specific

The opposite of this might be _____

How would my team benefit immediately if I applied this
coaching quality?

_____

_____

_____

5. Failure to secure commitment

The opposite of this might be _____

How would my team benefit immediately if I applied this
coaching quality?

_____

_____

_____

6. Taking the course of least resistance

The opposite of this might be _____

How would my team benefit immediately if I applied this
coaching quality?

_____

_____

_____

7. *Failure to identify results*

The opposite of this might be _____

How would my team benefit immediately if I applied this coaching quality?

_____

_____

_____

8. *Impatience*

The opposite of this might be _____

How would my team benefit immediately if I applied this coaching quality?

_____

_____

_____

WHAT TO EXPECT
WHEN YOU'RE DOING IT RIGHT

As an effective coach, you will begin to experience very specific, very real results — and results make coaching exciting. When you see people growing and changing, and you know you are contributing to that growth — that's one of the most exciting things that can happen to you as a manager and StaffCoach™.

As you recall, you should use your coaching role for people who are performing above their job standards. In the coaching role, your primary goals are to practice involvement that builds trust, clarify and verify your team communications, affirm, motivate and inspire. On the next page are some of the results you can expect to see when you are effectively performing that role.

- **Clarification of performance expectations**
- **Changes in point of view**
- **Increased self-sufficiency/autonomy**
- **Insight into behavior and feelings**
- **Acceptance of difficult tasks**

1. Clarification of performance expectations

When you properly perform the coaching role, both you and your team members have a clearer understanding of what performance is expected. Because you talk with your people, you have a clearer picture of what each can do. And they get a clearer picture of what you expect. Quite often, this increased communication inspires both of you to greater achievement.

2. Changes in point of view

Because you are involved, respectful of team-member opinions and affirming their skills and goals, you will learn more about the other person's point of view. And because you are encouraging and inspiring others, you will be *changing* their points of view — helping them catch a new and broader perspective and professional vision.

3. Increased self-sufficiency/autonomy

An important outcome of effective coaching is the increase in the self-sufficiency and autonomy of team members. Being coached should help give team members a freeing new identity ... a sense of importance. It imparts confidence. It gradually eliminates the individual's need to prove his worthiness. Instead, it allows team members to rechannel "ego-energy" into collective goals. Once team members are secure about how you view them ... and how they can perform ... they are ready to energize teammates who may not be as self-sufficient. If you coach a team like that, congratulations! You're doing exactly what a great coach is supposed to do!

Being coached should help give team members a sense of importance.

4. Insight into behavior and feelings

There's an important concept you need to understand as a coach: Thoughts become feelings and feelings become behavior. Sounds simple enough, but unless you are conscious of the process, you can fall into the habit of responding to people with emotional "knee jerks." You will be more likely to react negatively to the people who have typically been difficult — and more likely to react positively to those who haven't made waves. That can be very damaging to growth — yours and the team's.

Why? Because it reinforces the subconscious idea that people are valuable only when they perform at expected levels. And, as we've discussed, that kind of message does not "free" people to be people!

Here's a three-step process to monitor the "knee-jerk" response tendency:

When someone does or says something that bothers you, instead of blowing up, stop and take a deep breath. Then, ask yourself three questions:

- *"What part of this problem is the employee's and what part may be mine?"*
  For instance, have you ever been given "great" tickets to a sporting event, only to discover that you are much farther from the field or court than you imagined? You find yourself sitting there seething inwardly about the injustice of it all ... *even when the seats are free!*

  The same situation can occur in the work environment when team-member attitudes or actions conflict with your expectations. Someone's choice of clothing may seem inappropriate for a client presentation. Someone's phone manner may seem grating or insensitive. Maybe those observations are true and need to be addressed. But first examine yourself — avoid a "knee-jerk" response! You may find the difficulty lies in your negative expectations, not in the employee's actual behavior.

> **Thoughts become feelings and feelings become behavior.**

- **"What is the specific feeling that I'm choosing to feel because of this action?"**
  Note the key word, *"choosing."* You have the ability to reject or accept feelings. As a coach, you have the *responsibility* to do that!

- **"What is the root reason for my feelings?"**
  What lies at the core of your anger, frustration, disappointment or bitterness? Does it really bear on this specific action or does it have its roots in something totally unrelated?

None of us approaches any experience totally free of experiences that preceded it. And that's good. After all, if we didn't learn from bad experiences and use that knowledge to avoid repeating them, we would be in trouble. But, if we're not careful, we can also allow experiences from the past to hinder or prevent positive responses in the present.

The truth is, a bad haircut really *can* cause us to respond more negatively to people and events than we would normally. An unexplained dent in your new car *can* make you sound curt to a client on the phone. But, knowing that, a coach *must* evaluate his responses — otherwise, your team members will begin to feel like children waiting for Mom and Dad to be in a good mood before approaching them with something important.

Have you ever been upset and not really known why? Someone asks, "What's wrong?" and you say, "I don't know." And you really don't. You're not in control. When you ask yourself the three questions listed previously, you're getting yourself under control so you can talk to people as an adult and not as an irate parent trying to punish a child for doing something wrong. Act … don't react!

Act … don't react!

5. Acceptance of difficult tasks

There's one more outcome you can expect if you have effectively assumed the role of coach. Your team members will accept increasingly difficult tasks. This is a natural result of team members having a clearer understanding of your expectations — as well as the confidence to work more independently. And it's important for you, as a coach, to encourage that growth. Challenge your people. Let them know that you have confidence in them. Let them know you think they are "unlimited resources." Let them know you think they can do and be whatever they choose — and they will!

CASE STUDY

Nancy Evans joined the staff of a private Southern college as director of food services just three weeks after the former director had died suddenly in an automobile accident. When the associate director learned he would not be offered the vacated post, he resigned immediately. So Nancy took over a 37-person team with only four days to review records, accounts, menus and personnel files ... as well as inspect the campus food-service complex.

Her first act as director was to call a Saturday morning meeting (well before any of the food facilities were expected to be active) of the entire food-service staff to do five things:

1. Introduce herself
2. Assure everyone that someone was at the helm
3. Deal with rumors surrounding the associate director's resignation
4. Discuss her immediate goals
5. Answer any questions team members might have

After she covered her first three points, Nancy passed out a list of her short-term goals. She also placed them on an overhead projector while she spoke. Her goals were:

1. To meet with every employee in the next two weeks to discuss:
   a. The strengths and weaknesses of the school's food-service program from each employee's point of view
   b. The special concerns and dreams of each employee
   c. Ideas for growth — the employee's as well as the program's

2. To thoroughly familiarize herself with working environments in all five food-service outlets: the Student Union Cafeteria, the alum and faculty "Regency Restaurant" (also located in The Union), The Snack Shop and the two dormitory cafeterias — and to hold team meetings with the complete staffs of each.

3. To establish an Administrative Committee to function in the vacated role of associate director. The committee would be composed of the five current staff managers, plus three team-elected members. The duties of the committee were to be defined in upcoming brainstorming sessions.

The time Nancy had anticipated for the question session proved too short. Many members had questions. It was apparent that loyalties to the associate who resigned existed — as well as much anger at the president over treatment and salary issues.

Nancy noted each remark or complaint on overheads for all to see. By the time the session was over, she had 11 note-packed overhead transparencies! Nancy concluded the meeting by promising to transcribe each remark, to study each and to report her conclusions to everyone within one month.

The days ahead were busy ones for Nancy. She asked for and was given an office in the Student Union building instead of the office of the past director. She met daily with the five managers to discuss operations and to brainstorm methods to improve service and profitability.

She met daily with at least two members of the food-service team, with one during breakfast and the other over lunch, getting to know more about each, and generally covering the three areas she had outlined for them in her introductory meeting.

One month later, Nancy called another early morning team meeting. She opened that meeting by welcoming the "Food Brood." At that point, she turned the meeting over to the Food Service Administrative Committee, who passed out folders titled, *"Where We Are & Where We're Going ... Together!"* covering:

1. The new Committee-created Mission Statement
2. Ten new employee policies and benefits based on employee remarks in the introductory meeting
3. A new "profit sharing" bonus plan tied to each facility team's ability to create and implement new cost-saving, revenue-generating measures

Included in each folder was an "Impressions and Evaluations" form employees were encouraged to complete and return to their team leaders in one week.

Then the meeting was opened for questions. Committee members answered the surprisingly few questions that were asked. When it was apparent that there were no more questions, Nancy stood to conclude the meeting.

She began by requesting a round of applause for members of the Administrative Committee. It was their efforts, she assured the group, that made the many positive new steps a reality. Then she expressed her gratitude to the president, who had reviewed the entire plan just presented and had approved it wholeheartedly. She then thanked the entire group for the fun of working alongside them, for allowing her to get to know them and for the loyalty and commitment she saw in each person.

She concluded by telling the group that in only a short time every member had made her feel like "family."

CASE STUDY ANALYSIS

Nancy Evans demonstrated real coaching strengths in the scenario you just read. You get the feeling that her food-service team is going to benefit greatly from her leadership, don't you? Now let's focus on a few specifics that may give you deeper insights into the scenario — and into your own team/coach relationship.

1. What did the associate director's resignation tell you about the leadership style prior to Nancy's arrival? What message might the resignation have sent to the 37-member staff?

2. In her two total-team meetings, do you think Nancy communicated clearly? How?

3. Did she provide opportunities to verify employee understanding? How?

4. Was Nancy's choice of offices significant to you? Good or bad? Why?

5. Was Nancy's decision to have an Administrative Committee rather than an associate director a wise one? Why?

6. What other "involvement" steps did Nancy take in her coaching role?

7. Would the food-service team be motivated and inspired by the plans the Committee unveiled? Why or why not?

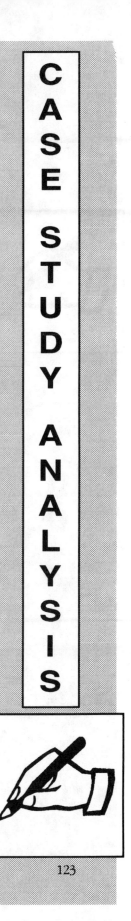

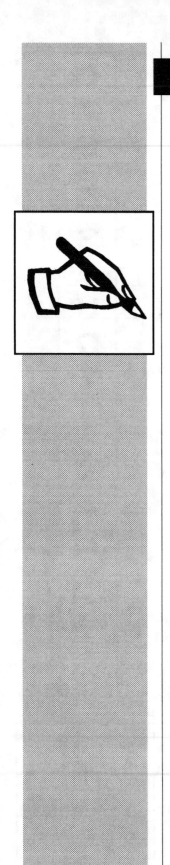

8. Do you think Nancy did anything to help eliminate resentment toward the president expressed in the first team meeting? Explain.

9. Do you think her concluding remarks about "family" were appropriate? Explain.

You may be thinking, "If only this coaching business was as easy to *do* as it is to *write* about." Agreed! But the encouraging fact is that real-life situations ... much more chaotic and potentially disastrous than Nancy's case study ... have been and are being handled capably by StaffCoaching™ principles. This is not pie-in-the-sky thinking — it can mean cake-in-the-plate results!

CHAPTER QUIZ

1. Which employees are the best candidates for the coaching role? Who would fit that description on your team?

2. What four key attributes characterize the coaching role?

3. Name four ways to establish coach/team-member trust. Which area are you weakest in?

4. What method of verifying your communication to the team appeals most to you? Which one haven't you tried?

5. Which method of affirming your team members would work best in your environment?

6. Name three non-monetary motivators from this chapter that you currently use.

The Mentoring Role: Instruction by Example

"Everything you say, and do, as well as everything you fail to say will communicate a message. You cannot NOT influence people!" — Jack Mackey

MAKING GREAT STRIDES BY "WALKING ALONGSIDE"

The mentoring role is reserved for managing a person whose performance is standard or average. While the catchwords for coaching are "inspire" and "motivate," the catchword for mentoring is "instruct." When you mentor, it's your job to teach new skills. Typically, that's the only way average performers can grow and begin experiencing improved performance.

Think of a mentor as a person who walks alongside someone else. In the mentoring role, you "come alongside" the people on your team. You work with them side by side, giving instruction — and not just *verbal* instruction. It's "hands-on" instruction. It's doing the task together. You lead by example.

> *Like it or not, you are the example.*

Jack Mackey founded and managed four restaurants and a full-line catering business — so he understands service. In 1988, Jack made a career move to become a trainer and consultant. He recently finished recording a training program entitled Customer Service System *for National Press Publications. He serves as Director of Business Training and Development Services at National Seminars Group, specializing in Customer Satisfaction, Total Quality Management and Leadership. He has successfully coached entry-level staff members, professional craftsmen and career managers.*

Why? One reason is that every team follows what its coach "models." If managers tell team members to come to work on time but come to work late themselves, what will team members do? Show up late, of course. Whatever the coach does, to a greater or lesser degree, team members will emulate. Like it or not, *you* are the example.

Besides instructing and leading by example, your other task as a mentor is to develop new abilities in the people you work with. You'll help people develop new skills ... help them do things they never knew they could do. You'll teach each person how to be more competent in more areas.

A PROCESS WITH PRODUCTIVE PURPOSE

The mentoring process demands a plan. It's a process of development ... not a practice of shooting from the hip. No leader arrives at work Monday morning and announces, "Guess what, today I'm going to mentor you." Instead, each mentor builds a plan — and for any plan to be successful, it must be built on three components:

- **Mutual trust and commitment**
- **Patient leadership**
- **Emotional maturity**

1. Mutual trust and commitment

Mutual trust and commitment between people come from spending time together. The more time you spend teaching someone, the more commitment you have to that person and she will have to you.

This should tell you something about the mentoring process in general. It is slow. Hard words to hear, perhaps, but nonetheless true. Some managers make the mistake of believing that their *intentions* to mentor are 90 percent of the battle, and that the other 10 percent involves the actual work.

Two dangers exist in harboring this illusion:

- When the truth hits home that the formula is actually reversed — 10 percent intention, 90 percent hands-on, day-to-day effort — some managers become so discouraged they never really get started. Which leads to the second danger ...

- The team member may perceive that she is not worth special attention and grows to distrust not only your motives, but eventually her own value and ability.

What's the point? Simply this: Mentoring is hard work and it takes time — but thousands of managers just like you have done it and *are* doing it with terrific results. Ask any of them if their commitment is a necessary element and if team-member trust is the result. What do you think they will answer? If you guessed "Absolutely," you're absolutely right.

2. Patient leadership

Patience is extremely important in the mentoring process. Once you've established the commitment and trust discussed above, you maintain it through patience. You will have plenty of opportunity to exercise patience. That's because people are ... well ... people. The need for patience will present itself in three basic areas:

- *Employee attentiveness*

    The things *you* think are important about certain concepts and procedures may not seem all that important to your "mentoree."

Example:

Coach:
The key to this phase of the job, Rob, is watching this set of figures here. They will tell you instantly if this product is safe to send on ahead. Do you understand that?

Rob:
Sure. Where does that door lead?

> *"Why can't we have patience and expect good things to take time?"*
>
> *—John Wooden*

Coach:

What door? Oh — well, it leads to the equipment lockers. But about these figures I was discussing — you're sure you have a clear grasp of ...

Impatience would tempt *anyone* to say something like, "Earth to Rob: Wake up ... this process is *lots* more important than where a dumb door goes!" But remember, your mentoree's perceived response to information may have no bearing whatsoever on how well she processes it. And, more importantly, it may be totally unlike your own. No one will ever mirror your values or priorities perfectly. Don't expect it.

Naturally, if inattentiveness becomes a real problem, you will have to deal with it — but be ready to exercise patience by giving your mentoree the benefit of the doubt.

• *Employee aptitude*

Some people learn faster than others. As obvious as that may sound, it is hard to remember it in a mentoring situation. Your mentoree may be way ahead of your most "difficult" explanations ... finishing sentences for you ... evidencing an advanced grasp of concepts it took you much longer to "own." More likely, however, she may require very precise, step-by-step explanations from you in order to effectively apply information in an actual work situation. Your two key jobs as a mentor in this area are to:

(1) Evaluate the team member's understanding with questions like, "Is there anything I've said that could be a little clearer?" or "If you were explaining this to someone else, how would you do it?"

(2) Encourage your mentoree to feel perfectly comfortable asking questions by *telling* him or her to feel that way ... and by responding maturely when the questions come.

Some people learn faster than others.

Fast learner or not-so-fast learner, your mentoree can learn from your patient approach to her training needs.

- ***Pressure to attend to "business as usual"***

Let's face it. Finding time in your already overcrowded schedule to mentor one or more team members will take some doing. But it can be done. Thousands of successful coaches are making it happen. One way many do it is represented by the simple but effective "15-5-10" Formula:

- **15**
Rank your daily duties in order of importance and break out the bottom 15 percent.

- **5**
Delegate that 15 percent to selected team members, using 5 percent of the time you saved to continue directing them and reviewing their work.

- **10**
Use the remaining 10 percent for mentoring activities.

And where does patience come into play in this area? The inclination to resent or begrudge the time you spend away from "normal" job activities will grow as you progress in your mentoring projects. It's a natural tendency. You will be tempted to postpone or skip mentoring opportunities in the interest of "more important things." When that happens, remember:

(1) You aren't "losing" time while you mentor — you're using *free* time made available because you delegated duties.

(2) Your mentoree will know in a minute if you view your time with her as a time-wasting inconvenience.

So have patience with the mentoring process. It will pay off!

The "15-5-10" Formula

3. Emotional maturity

Additionally, an effective mentor (or any other leader, for that matter) is able to control her emotions for the sake of effective leadership. Even when you're sick of hearing the same questions over and over again, you must remain (or *appear* to remain) calm and eager to help.

How do you do that? Volumes have been written dealing with the issue of emotional control. There are nearly as many methods as there are managers — but here are three that continue to deliver results for managers in a wide variety of organizational environments:

- *See the mentoree as your child.*

  Everyone is someone's child. So when the questions seem especially irrelevant ... when your tendency to explode or give up seems impossible to push down ... think how the mentoree's parents would want you to react. Think how you would want a manager to respond if the mentoree was *your* child, or your brother or sister, etc. Silly? Try it anyway. You will be surprised at the effect the exercise has on your attitudes and responses.

- *Schedule mentoring sessions to end with "rewards."*

  Having something to look forward to can minimize emotional intensity. Anger is less likely to grip a person who is about to do something pleasurable. So schedule your mentoring sessions to end with lunch or quitting time, etc. Not because your mentoring sessions will be dreary, painful experiences — they won't be. But they *can* be demanding and a bit draining, as any good teacher will tell you. So anticipate the possibility of frayed nerves and prepare for them. Then you can tell your emotions that "recess" is coming soon.

Always remain calm and eager to help.

- ***Speak with a smile***

  Emotional upheaval is usually accompanied by raised
  voices and "strained" facial features (frowns, etc.).
  Anger, fear, and indignation are virtually impossible to
  express (for long) with a smiling face and soft,
  conversational tones. Moral: When emotions threaten
  to distort your normally mature responses, take a deep
  breath ... consciously speak more softly ... and smile!
  It does more than hide inner turmoil. It actually
  defuses it!

  In Uganda, farmers pair the young beginner ox with
  an older ox. The two oxen are tied together with a
  special harness. The device is called a training yoke —
  and it is configured to make sure the older ox pulls
  most of the burden. The older ox has the control. If
  the farmers don't do that, the younger ox tends to go
  too fast or too slow. The older ox has the control, so
  it'll go at the right pace. The younger one must work
  at the same pace. The young ox learns from the
  experience of "walking alongside." Can you see the
  wisdom in that from a mentoring standpoint? If you've
  never mentored before, keep this illustration in mind
  in the days and years ahead. It will begin to have
  special relevance as you interact with mentorees.

> *"Soft words bring
> hard things to
> pass."*
>
> *— Aesop*

THE SIX WAYS PEOPLE THINK

As we discussed at the start of this chapter, one of the main
reasons for mentoring someone is to instruct her. For that
reason, the impact of your mentoring will depend on how well
you are able to teach. And how well you are able to teach
depends on how well you understand how adults learn. If
every adult learned exactly the same way, your job might not
be especially challenging. But the truth is everyone learns
differently!

The learning process depends on how people accept or
receive knowledge. So every mentor must understand the six
basic ways people think. None of these ways is necessarily

better or worse than the others. They are just different. It's important for you as a StaffCoach™ to remember not to judge people by the way they think. Instead, you need to learn as much as possible about the *way* they think and, therefore, how you can best motivate them to learn.

- **Authority-driven**
- **Deductive**
- **Sensory**
- **Emotional**
- **Intuitive**
- **Scientific**

1. Authority-driven thinkers

Some people accept and process knowledge best by taking specific direction from authority. If you mentor these people, all you usually have to do is tell them to do something. You're the boss. They'll do it. Many coaches prefer this kind of employee. Such a person rarely talks back or questions orders. Those can be commendable characteristics, but remember also that problems can arise in dealing with people who respond to authority with "knee-jerk" obedience. They may do whatever you tell them to do, but sometimes they don't do anything *unless* you tell them.

Your task is to recognize where that line of motivation exists within each authority-driven team member, and to help her recognize it, too.

Example:

Coach:
Jim, this newsletter headline is the old one. Didn't you substitute the emergency headline change I gave you yesterday?

Jim:
I rushed it to the editorial department like you said. I even did it on my lunch hour.

Authority-driven thinkers may not do anything unless you tell them.

Coach:
And?

Jim:
And, let's see … I put it in Carla's in-box. Was that wrong?

Coach:
The newsletter was already on the press. That headline had to be added before the run started!

Jim:
Wow.

Coach:
"Wow" is right. But the good news is the press broke down. They only ran off a few copies like this one. So take this new headline to editorial now and we still have time to correct it.

Jim:
You bet!

Coach:
And, Jim … what do you think is the best way to use this time?

Jim:
I'll make sure the press people know we're altering the plates, and then I'll go straight to typesetting.

Coach:
Great thinking. Go for it!

2. Deductive thinkers

The second way people accept or process facts is through deductive reasoning. When you mentor people whose minds work this way, you must make things logical. These people prefer linear, analytical explanations — point A to point B. You have to go into detail … sometimes almost defending your own thought processes. These people have to understand each step. When you stop and say, "OK, now you go ahead and do it," they'll probably say, "Can you run through that one

Deductive thinkers have to understand each step.

more time, please?" If you're a "Type A" personality, these deductive team members will test your patience threshold! You will be tempted to shout, "I told you twice! Why do I have to tell you again?" But they're not doing it to upset you. They truly need to understand. Now the good news: Once they *do* understand a task, they'll know it forever!

3. Sensory thinkers

A third way people learn is through sensory experience. These are "hands-on" people. They have to see it, hear it, touch it. They have to go through the full experience. Only then will they "own" the process with you. To best mentor sensory-oriented people, give them the time they need to explore. Encourage them to touch and feel, and they will learn faster.

Example:

> *Coach*:
> What do you think? Great piece of equipment, isn't it?
>
> *Mentoree*:
> It sure is. And you were right about not trying to punch out more than three shapes. I tried four and it only partially punched the last one.
>
> *Coach*:
> You did? Well, don't try punching faster than I *showed* you. It can cause metal to bunch up and splinter on down the line.
>
> *Mentoree:*
> It must not cause that *every* time.
>
> *Coach*:
> You tried that, too?
>
> *Mentoree*:
> Yes.
>
> *Coach*:
> Well, I'm glad I didn't tell you not to try anything else!

Sensory thinkers are "hands-on" people.

136

4. Emotional thinkers

Some minds let in information primarily through emotions. These people need to "feel good" about the work experience ... about the job process ... about their skills ... about the task outcome. If they don't, their performance will soon show it. You can often motivate emotionally responsive team members by understanding that each human being responds to one of four basic emotional needs:

- ### *The need for control*

  Some team members respond poorly to assignments unless they feel in control of their environment. If they aren't in control, they grow uncomfortable. The way to assure someone that she is in control is to point to her "win" record. Show these team members how they are doing ... how they contribute productively. Those things all verify "control."

  ### Example:

  Diane:
  I've just got writer's block, I guess. I can't seem to come up with any sell lines I like.

  Coach:
  Well, let's brainstorm some solutions together. Point-of-purchase signage for stuffed farm animals shouldn't be too tough to have some fun with.

  Diane:
  It's not that. It's just that by the time the designers get finished with it, who knows if anyone will read it?

  Coach:
  What makes you say that? The last series you did pulled in great sales. The artists designed directly to your words.

> *Emotional thinkers need to feel good about the job.*

Diane:
That time, maybe. But you never know.

Coach:
What I *do* know is that your words start the whole process. Without that those signs are just so much wallpaper. And I know something else.

Diane:
What?

Coach:
You and I can't draw a straight line — so we better get busy and do what we *can* do. Write!

- ### *The need for attention*

  Some people won't respond very long to anything if they don't get positive attention from it. Not that they must constantly be "in the spotlight" — they simply need to know that their contributions are consistently appreciated. They need a clear cause-and-effect relationship between good performance and favorable reviews.

- ### *The need for love*

  Many people must know that the leader cares about them personally as well as professionally. These people are motivated by knowing that the coach sees "special" attributes in their characters or abilities. They need to feel that the leader is grateful for them and for the type of employee they are. Most people demonstrate this need to some degree. The downside of this need? Delivering criticism to people who need to feel cared for is a sensitive challenge. Use much tact, time and tenderness when correction is in order for these team members.

It is more important to be human than to be important.

- ### *The need for justice or "rightness"*

  You will occasionally manage people who won't do anything unless it's "correct" — organizationally or culturally proper. These folks are much like the "deductive reasoners" you learned about earlier. "Why aren't you doing the job?" you might ask one of these people. "I didn't know if I should — I didn't know if it was right," they may respond. These people are not going to budge until they feel that the task lines up with written and even unwritten policy. Once you assure them that the procedure is organizationally correct (and, if necessary, ethically correct), they will respond eagerly and well.

  When you deal with a person who is primarily motivated by emotion, find a way to tap into one of her basic needs. You'll likely find the results you want.

5. Intuitive thinkers

The fifth way people assimilate data is by intuition. Intuition is an unconscious process that is neither rational nor emotional. Have you ever worked on something all day that didn't "click," somehow? You didn't quite get it. Then you went to bed that evening, ill at ease about the day's unsettling activity. But the next morning you woke up and … eureka! … you had the answer.

That's an aspect of intuition. While you sleep, your unconscious mind still processes information. Sometimes it wakes you in the middle of the night with the right answer. When you mentor people who operate by intuition, you have to give them time to grasp things. Tell them, "Hey, sleep on it. We'll look at it tomorrow. No problem." You may be surprised at the number of "eureka" moments these people experience.

> *Intuitive thinkers experience "eureka" moments.*

6. Scientific thinkers

The last way people process information is scientifically. To mentor these people means letting them test it, try it, experiment with it. They have to explore the information scientifically. Until they do that, your counsel is often just so much theory to them. For example, let's say you're teaching them a new computer program. If you say, "Whatever you do, don't do that. If you do, it will erase everything," they will probably respond with something like, "How do you know?" You might say, "Well, it happened to *me*. I did that and everything was gone." Don't be surprised if they come back with, "Maybe it's changed. Maybe something is different now and it doesn't work that way." A word of advice: Save yourself some headaches and let these people experiment and try out their own theories. Set up safe situations for them to satisfy their curiosity.

How will you find out the ways your people respond to information? Observe and ask questions. The following questions can generate responses that help you evaluate which "thinker type" each team member you mentor might be. While almost all of us are combinations of the six types, usually one approach will dominate our thought patterns.

STYLE ANALYSIS QUESTIONS

- Does this phase of the job make sense to you?

- Does any part of the task seem unnecessary?

- Would you call this task hard? Easy? Why?

- What might you do differently to streamline the task?

- Is there anything that might better equip you to do the task?

- What part of the task appeals most to you? Least? Why?

Scientific thinkers must test their own theories.

THE THREE KEY PHASES
OF SUCCESSFUL MENTORING

Do you remember classes in school where you sat for what seemed like hours and repeated facts over and over? How many of those facts do you remember today? For that matter, how many of those facts did you remember two weeks after you were tested on them? Not many? Join the crowd!

The reason you don't remember them is because you were only *told* facts. You weren't *shown* how those truths could be applied in your daily life. And you weren't asked to apply that information *yourself.* An example of the best kind of learning we experienced as children is the art of tying a shoe. We were first *told* that tied shoes made our feet feel better and lessened the chance of tripping over loose laces ... then were carefully *shown* how to tie those laces ... and finally we were supervised as *we* tied our own shoe laces. Result? Information we have "owned" since preschool —and will *always* own.

True learning works the same way with adults. When you *tell* an adult how to do something, she will remember 10 percent of what you say. If you *show* an adult how to do something, she will remember 60 percent. But If you *do* something with that same adult, she will remember 90 percent ... or more.

It's amazing:

> *Adults will remember 10 percent of what they hear, 60 percent of what they see and 90 percent of what they do!*

Based on those facts, what do you think is the best way to teach an adult? By having her do tasks. But what is the *usual* way we teach adults? We tell them. And what happens? Adults learn, but only at a fraction of their capacity.

The three phases of the mentoring process use the "10-60-90" Principle just discussed to instruct people so they will learn and grow to their greatest potential in the least amount of time. As a StaffCoach™ in the mentoring role, you'll use these three phases whenever you teach your people.

The "10-60-90" Principle

Three Phases of Mentoring

> PHASE 1 — Observe
> PHASE 2 — Participate
> PHASE 3 — Conduct

1. Observe

In the first phase, the person you teach observes you doing the job. As she watches you do the job, you should be answering questions. You need to answer these questions, even if they aren't asked outright:

- *Why is this job important?*
- *What are the key components of this job?*
- *What are the cautions?*
- *What timing issues are important?*
- *What's in this for me?*

Example:

Coach:
Well, what did you think of your first sales meeting, Phyllis? Pretty wild, huh?

Phyllis:
Yes, but you handled it well. I just hope I can do it half as well when the time comes.

Coach:
What part of it seemed the most difficult to you?

Phyllis:
Just hearing so many problems or objections that you have to have answers for. I'm not sure I could do that.

Coach:
Sure you could. All of the problems the sales team expressed today dealt with two basic areas: existing product pricing and dealer service issues. The key to solving those problems is knowing why prices are the way they are and what programs are in place, or coming, to maintain quality service — and how we compare with competition.

> "That is happiness: to be dissolved into something complete and great."
>
> — Willa Cather

142

Phyllis:
Oh, is *that* all!

Coach:
It may sound like a lot, but you'll have all the research you need to know those things very well, and well in advance. Plus I'm confident that you can do it at least as well … maybe better.

Phyllis:
I don't know. Some of those guys were pretty irritated — and they've been around a long time.

Coach:
True. I've just learned not to take anything said in those meetings personally, and not to feel as if I have to leave with everyone liking me.

Phyllis:
They seemed to respect you.

Coach:
If they do, it's because I know they need to hear the truth — even when it's not what they want to hear. I just stick to the truth. Sometimes it's good news, sometimes it's not. But my mother always told me "never alter the truth to make short-term friends, and you'll never have long-term enemies." It's a good thing to remember in sales meetings.

Phyllis:
I'll remember.

Earlier you read about the importance of communicating with your people. As you show them how to do the job, you add significance to the task … you communicate your own mastery of and respect for the task. You make the mentoree feel that she is doing a job you and the organization consider meaningful.

A common mistake mentors make in this phase is going through the job too quickly. If you rush your demonstration of the job, the learner doesn't have a chance to absorb what's going on — to ask the questions she may

Don't rush your demonstration of the job.

143

need to ask. Hurrying also leaves the learner with the impression that neither the job nor the worker is really worth your time. Slow down while you demonstrate the task. Allow the learner to see every aspect of the job and to ask questions. And maintain a relaxed, friendly attitude — even if you have to repeat the task two or three times.

Why? Think for a moment about the teachers and "inspirers" you identified back in Chapter 1 (page 20). What made them so good? What made it easy, even fun, to learn from them? Chances are your answer will be something like, "I knew I could try and fail and try again without feeling foolish or worthless." No one enjoys learning with the threat of time or performance minimums hanging over her head. Give your mentoree time to learn, and she will give you many reasons to be glad you did.

2. Participate

After you've demonstrated the job, the next phase is to have the team member do the job with you. This second phase of teaching an adult to do a task involves three points:

> *To teach is to learn twice.*

* *How can the task be shared?*

    First, determine how the task can be shared. You'll both be doing part of it. It's up to you to determine how the process can be shared meaningfully and memorably. Generally, it's a good idea to allow the mentoree to assist in the task while you perform the task essentials — not vice versa. This allows a beginning person more freedom to learn ... less pressure to "get it right" the first time. For instance, if you were helping your mentoree learn how to paint a wall, her part of the the task might be holding the ladder, keeping the brushes clean, etc.

    Occasionally, a task is so tied to single-operator functions that the mentoree can only look on while the mentor performs it, but those situations are rare.

How about you? List below the tasks that persons you might mentor could participate in while learning from your performance.

MENTOREE'S NAME	TASK TO SHARE	MENTOREE'S ASSISTANT JOB	COACH'S ROLE AS TEACHER

As discussed earlier in this chapter (pages 133-140), people will begin to demonstrate what "thinker type" they are in these learning situations. If you sense the mentoree's need for a more "deductive" or "scientific" (or whatever) teaching style, you can tailor your instructions to that style and thereby facilitate the learning experience.

- ***Does the mentoree understand?***

  Next, make sure the learner demonstrates understanding. How do you know when a person has adequately learned the task? One obvious way is to ask! Determine how much the person understands about the task by asking her to explain it to you ... or even better, to someone else.

• **_Is there time to learn?_**

Allow plenty of time for instruction. As in the first phase, don't rush the process ... don't make the learner feel under time pressure to complete the task. Allow time for the training to be done well.

3. Conduct

Once you've done the task with your mentoree, it's time for her to fly solo. There are four questions that you, as a mentor/instructor, must resolve before you begin the conducting stage.

• **How can the student demonstrate competency?**

• **What level of competency will be adequate?**

• **How much inaccuracy will be allowed?**

• **When will unsupervised work be allowed?**

a. How can the student demonstrate competency?

In most job environments, the answer to this question will probably be something fairly subjective like, "When the manager is convinced." Much of the time that response is probably fine. Being "convinced" usually means the mentoree appears comfortable with the task activities and the skill level required and grasps the logic behind the order of activities, etc. Additionally, no major mentoree questions remain unanswered ... no fears or confusion are evident.

But, for other environments, where safety or secrecy issues are of special concern, written tests may be necessary to answer this question to the satisfaction of all.

b. What level of competency will be adequate?

What specific things *must* occur for you to feel satisfied
that the student has truly mastered the job? Are these
specific things time related? Quality related? Quantity
related? If answers to these questions are critical to proper
job performance, they should be formalized and made
known to the mentoree in advance. Making sure questions
like these are answered positively will affect the amount of
time you spend modeling a task for the mentoree, as well
as the sense of urgency associated with the mentoring
process.

c. How much inaccuracy will be allowed?

When people are first learning a job, they will make
mistakes. How many mistakes are acceptable? What kind?
No person or book (outside your own organization) can
answer these questions for you — but they must be
resolved. Otherwise the teaching process is an
independent, irrelevant exercise for all involved. Without
some performance benchmark, however minimal, words
like "quality" and "improvement" become subjective.

d. When will unsupervised work be allowed?

When will you lessen your supervision of the person and
allow her to be more independent? What might be the
price of letting the student work unassisted? Can you
afford it?

Again, these questions demand the development of
general guidelines for every organizational task your
mentoree might attempt. The form that follows is one way
to help make that process possible.

*If at first you
don't succeed,
you are in the
majority.*

JOB PHASE PROGRESS REPORT

TASK _____ TITLE_____ DATE BEGUN_____ DATE ENDED_____
STUDENT _____ COACH_____ DEPT. _____

1. OBSERVING THE TASK	COMPREHENSION AND COMPETENCE	ADDITIONAL DEVELOPMENT NEEDS	MANAGER'S REMARKS
	SAT. GOOD EXCEL.		
_____			
_____			
_____			
_____			

2. PARTICIPATING IN THE TASK	COMPREHENSION AND COMPETENCE	ADDITIONAL DEVELOPMENT NEEDS	MANAGER'S REMARKS
	SAT. GOOD EXCEL.		
_____			
_____			
_____			

3. CONDUCTING THE TASK	COMPREHENSION AND COMPETENCE	ADDITIONAL DEVELOPMENT NEEDS	MANAGER'S REMARKS
	SAT. GOOD EXCEL.		
_____			
_____			
_____			

Phase 1: The learner watches
Phase 2: You do the job together
Phase 3: You watch the learner do the job

It's the "10-60-90" Principle in action!

After reviewing these three phases, what do you think you need most to mentor someone? If you said "time," you're a fast learner! This point can't be emphasized too much. If you're mentoring the right way, you'll have moments when you become very frustrated. You'll think, "This is taking way too much time — how can I keep doing this and my own job, too?"

Be ready for those moments. Work through them by implementing the "15-5-10" Formula discussed earlier on page 131, and by remembering that mentoring can be effective only one way: by taking the mentor's time. It takes time to develop team members. And, after all, what other job is more important for a StaffCoach™ than developing team members?

THE OUTCOME OF EFFECTIVE MENTORING

If you do your job as a mentor well, what kind of outcomes can you expect? Your people will begin to show:

- Awareness of organizational politics and culture
- Appreciation of networking
- "Pro-active" approaches to their tasks
- Eagerness to learn
- Movement toward "expert" status
- Attitude of "advocacy"

1. Awareness of organizational politics and culture

In any organization, a lot goes on that isn't listed in the employee handbook. By mentoring a person whose performance is average, you can help her avoid being stymied by office politics. You can teach the person through your actions a consciousness of "accepted" activities she could not learn otherwise — like who to approach with certain problems or questions and who not to, and when and where certain

What do you need most to mentor someone? Time.

activities may or may not be "the norm." This doesn't mean teaching the person how to play games or how to "get around" organizational structure. On the contrary, it's like introducing a tourist to a foreign country. Nothing works better in learning an organization's culture than a guided tour by a "native."

In short, you can help your people understand what they have to know to prosper and grow in your special organizational culture and political environment.

2. Appreciation of networking

Mentoring properly must mean helping people see the value of "networking." Not just the benefits of exchanging business cards everywhere they go, or attending meetings of professional clubs to raise their industry or local-business exposure. Those things have their place in the broader context of networking, but they have little practical application in the context of day-to-day performance or productivity goals. Networking in this instance means helping your mentoree recognize and learn from the people in your organization most likely to help her grow professionally.

Help your people understand that interactivity and idea exchange with others is key to growth ... theirs and the team's! Maybe that means scheduling time for the team member to meet with someone in the organization who once had her job. It may mean introducing your mentoree to the department head in charge of jobs coming to your department — or in charge of jobs coming *from* your area. As your mentoree develops an understanding of and appreciation for the "big picture," her value to the organization will increase dramatically.

Teaching your mentoree about your office's politics is like introducing a tourist to a foreign country.

3. "Pro-active" approaches to their tasks

No team or team member can "rest on their laurels" or become content with business as usual and hope to experience significant increases in productivity. That's why you must inspire the people you mentor to become "pro-active" (as opposed to reactive) about the jobs they perform. One excellent way to communicate this mindset is by practicing what management expert Tom Peters calls the "one-idea club." A one-idea club is basically the practice of two or more people meeting to analyze a competitor's approach to business. The object is to find at least *one idea* the competitor is doing better — an idea that you might be able to use in your own environment.

Here's what you will discover. As your mentoree completes this process, with you or others, her inclination for productivity will increase. Why? Because as you go through that process, your mentoree will become more sensitive to learning. She will look at the work environment with new insights. You'll begin to hear things like, "You know, if we did this, it might help us in this area over here." Or, "If we changed this way of working, we would probably improve that situation." And when you can help that happen, you have just given your mentoree a lifetime gift.

CASE STUDY

Muriel and Jeff Havens owned a small business in rural Nebraska outside Omaha called "The Berry Bucket." They and the families of their three sons tended 20 acres of blackberries, blueberries and raspberries. The business attracted a good number of seasonal berry-picking customers, but had not grown substantially in over five years — in spite of increased advertising and new acreage (acquired by filling two of their six ponds) planted in boysenberries.

To continue to support the growing Havens clan, "The Berry Bucket" had to generate new dollars. At a monthly family meeting, it was suggested that perhaps the family business needed outside ideas. Each adult employee of

**C
A
S
E

S
T
U
D
Y**

the business was given the assignment of meeting with at least one person who currently operated a successful business, with the purpose of collecting advice that could translate into business growth for "The Berry Bucket."

Over the next month, six business CEOs were consulted. The businesses represented and the ideas gleaned from each are listed below:

Business	Advice
Flower and garden center	Move "The Berry Bucket" into Omaha and sell berry plants as well as berries.
Savings and loan	Offer gift certificates for pre-picked pints of berries, as well as for pies.
Greeting card shop	Add a gift store to the property to include local craft offerings.
Auto dealership	Offer a delivery service to the city for customers and small grocery stores.
Shopping mall	Develop year-round attractions like ice skating on frozen ponds, fairs, etc.
Marketing firm	Create a line of berry preserves with a new logo and label to test regionally.

In less than three years after their decision to solicit outside ideas, the Havens' business income had increased 600 percent. A gift shop employed five additional people. Four acres of spruce and pine Christmas trees surrounded three skating ponds. And their line of "The Berry Bucket" Homemade Jams was selling well in two states. Income from customers who came only to pick berries now constituted less than 50 percent of their profits.

Asked if she would recommend looking outside one's own work environment for new business ideas, Mrs. Havens said, "Only if you're ready to grow."

4. Eagerness to learn

Make sure your mentorees become avid and ongoing learners. Teach them to value and seek additional training — on their own or through the company. Dozens of public seminar firms offer one-day training programs on hundreds of topics that can start your people on new roads to effective time management, problem-solving, goal-setting, etc. Many on-site educational firms will bring training tailored to the needs you identify into your organization. Local junior colleges, colleges and private educational institutions offer evening classes that can provide needed skills inexpensively. However you choose to undergird your mentorees educationally, nothing will better assure your team's ongoing growth than developing "professional students"!

5. Movement toward "expert" status

Effective mentoring results in the learner moving toward expert status. As people learn, they will become more than skilled professionals — they will start to become specialists. By being mentored, people learn not only what they know, but what the person mentoring them knows, as well. It is an invaluable education process that paved the way for historical concepts like "apprenticeship." That concept transformed American business 200 years ago — and it can still do so today!

6. Attitude of "advocacy"

Whenever you mentor people, it shows an attitude of advocacy on your part. It shows that you are on their side — that you want them to succeed. And the wonderful thing about this attitude is that it's contagious. People who have been mentored are more likely to mentor others. And so the circle grows.

CASE STUDY

153

EFFECTIVE MENTORING WORKSHEET

In the spaces provided under the six outcomes of effective mentoring, answer the questions:

1. *Awareness of organizational politics and culture*
   In what way is my mentoring resulting in this benefit?
   _____

   What specific action could I take to assure growth in this area in 30 days?
   _____

2. *Appreciation of networking*
   In what way is my mentoring resulting in this benefit?
   _____

   What specific action could I take to assure growth in this area in 30 days?
   _____

3. *Pro-active approaches to their tasks*
   In what way is my mentoring resulting in this benefit?
   _____

   What specific action could I take to assure growth in this area in 30 days?
   _____

4. *Eagerness to learn*
   In what way is my mentoring resulting in this benefit?
   _____

   What specific action could I take to assure growth in this area in 30 days?
   _____

5. *Movement toward "expert" status*
   In what way is my mentoring resulting in this benefit?
   _____

   What specific action could I take to assure growth in this area in 30 days?
   _____

6. *Attitude of "advocacy"*
   In what way is my mentoring resulting in this benefit?
   _____

   What specific action could I take to assure growth in this area in 30 days?
   _____

THE TREASURE OF MENTORING

If you've participated in the mentoring process, you know that it never really stops. The people who mentored you probably have an honored place in your memory and life — just as you will for those you mentor. Mentors are *always* mentors in the minds of those they help.

In many ways, mentoring is the fulcrum on which the roles of "coach" and "counselor" balance. Without the investment of time, sweat and commitment inherent in the role of mentor, coaching and counseling would be less credible. It is far easier to motivate or correct someone who has known you to be a sincere, caring and patient teacher.

Your willingness to invest yourself in the life of another person will be the key that unlocks a treasure of fulfillment and accomplishment for many people ... beginning with you!

Mentors are always mentors in the minds of those they help.

155

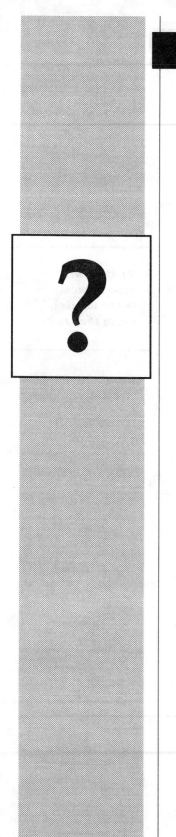

CHAPTER QUIZ

1. On what three components are good mentoring relationships built?

2. Name two of three ways to remain in control emotionally when mentoring.

3. What is the "15-5-10" Formula?

4. What are the six ways people think?

5. What are four "needs" that drive team members who are emotional thinkers?

6. Explain the "10-60-90" Principle.

7. Name the three phases of mentoring.

8. Who is the person on your team most likely to need mentoring?

CHAPTER 5

The Counseling Role: Confrontation and Correction

"Negative behavior, never confronted, never changes."   *— Jim Siress*

FOUR KEYS TO EFFECTIVE COUNSELING

The word "counseling" in the StaffCoaching™ Model doesn't mean psychological therapy. It means confronting and correcting people whose performance is below standard. When you deal with people who are not performing at an acceptable level, you *must* counsel them.

What constitutes "substandard performance"? The answer will vary, but substandard performance generally means:

> *Ongoing attitudes or actions that willfully or ignorantly fall short of stated, written or modeled duties.*

* Have the employee's duties been clearly communicated with reasonable frequency?

Jim Siress' background includes more than 20 years as a specialist in management and supervisory training. Jim studied psychology at Washington University and spent 13 years in management for Trans World Airlines. He has been a counselor in crisis-intervention programs for teenagers and has co-authored Coaching and Counseling for Bank Executives *for the American Bankers Association.*

When people are not performing at an acceptable level, you must counsel them.

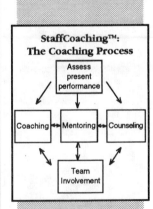

157

- Is the employee's behavior willfully or ignorantly inadequate toward these duties?

- Is the behavior ongoing?

If you answer "yes" to these questions (and assuming your criteria for "standard" performance are achievable by most people), the employee in question is probably operating at a substandard level.

Notice that "ignorance" (improper or inadequate awareness of job duties) may temporarily excuse substandard behavior ... especially if the opportunity to learn has not been properly offered or presented. But lack of knowledge should only raise the training level, never lower the standard of performance.

Counseling has four key phases:

1. ***Get and give information***
In this phase, the counselor gathers relevant information from the team member and, in return, responds to the person's need to receive information.

2. ***Agree on performance standards***
Obviously, to perform at a "standard" level for a specified task, each team member must understand and agree with the organizational definition of "standard." The counselor's job is to communicate that standard in a way the team member can understand and explain. How can you get valid agreement? Ask questions:

- *Do you fully understand the demands of this job?*
- *Is there any aspect of your job duties that could use some clarification?*
- *Do these activities seem doable to you?*
- *Is there anything you feel you might lack in order to do this task properly?*
- *How would you explain this task and the reason for it to a new employee?*

3. ***Correct***
The counselor implements the measures discussed to correct the performance and raise it to (or above) an acceptable standard. Remember that correcting people isn't a bad thing. It helps them become more productive ... more fulfilled.

4. *Refer*

The counselor refers the employee to the resources needed to improve his performance. Referral is crucial to performance change. Counselors don't just tell people their faults and leave it at that. They point employees to the tools (people or processes) that offer real opportunities to change and win. In order to do that effectively, a counselor must know where to point!

In some instances, effective referral may mean enrollment in a class or seminar, inside or outside the organization. It may mean asking another employee to mentor the team member in question — with special emphasis on the performance issue at hand. It does not mean disposing of the team member by pushing him off on someone else. *The counselor's responsibility for the team member's growth is furthered ... not finished ... by referral.*

To better equip themselves as counselors, some leaders listen regularly to training tapes. Some read one or two books a month on subjects relevant to the managerial challenges they face, like conflict management, empowerment or team-building. They do these things to stay ahead of the potential needs of the people on their teams — to be able to offer timely solutions to team-member challenges.

Example:

Bev:
I know what you're going to say: I'm doing a lousy job.

Coach:
No, I wasn't going to say that!

Bev:
You weren't?

Coach:
Of course not. I was going to ask you if there was any aspect of the job I could help you with.

Bev:
Same thing.

> *Most problems are little more than the absence of ideas.*

Coach:

It really isn't the same thing, Bev. I know you wouldn't do a "lousy job." A lousy job is when you know what to do but choose not to do it. That's not you. So what's the problem?

Bev:

I just can't seem to get my part of the assembly done on time. I don't know why. I try but I can't.

Coach:

What part of the job do you need more time with?

Bev:

I think there's plenty of time to do the job. I see others doing it. I just get flustered or something when I see my quotas start to fall behind. I wish I was as fast as Larry.

Coach:

I'll tell you what — do you know Linda in Shipping?

Bev:

Sure.

Coach:

Well, she trained Larry about a year before you came. I'm going to ask her if she'll come up here over lunch break tomorrow and tell you what she knows. Are you available over lunch tomorrow?

Bev:

Yes. That would be great.

Coach:

Linda is a great teacher. She'll know how to help. Then we'll talk afterwards. OK?

Why grin and bear it when you can smile and change it?

A winning coach gets that way by investing the time necessary to find and give the information that produces winning results!

THE PHILOSOPHY OF CONFRONTATION:
A POSITIVE APPROACH TO NEGATIVE EVENTS

In your role as counselor, you will have to confront inappropriate behavior. If you hate confrontation (and many of us do), you may have trouble with this role. If you aren't an assertive person, you will struggle at first. But you *must* struggle — and you can win!

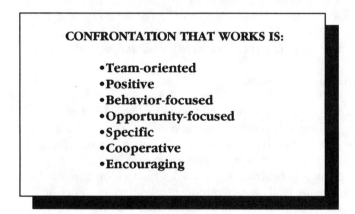

CONFRONTATION THAT WORKS IS:

- **Team-oriented**
- **Positive**
- **Behavior-focused**
- **Opportunity-focused**
- **Specific**
- **Cooperative**
- **Encouraging**

Team-oriented

A counselor must learn to say, "Terry, we have a problem." Not "Terry, YOU have a problem," or "Terry, you ARE a problem," or "Terry, I have a problem." It is always "our" problem. Why? Because you operate within a *team*. You're working together toward common goals ... toward better results.

Positive

Many counselors find it helpful to remember that confrontation is not negative. Confrontation is a *positive* approach to negative events. When you think of confrontation, you shouldn't cringe. Why? Because the StaffCoaching™ Model is based on the concept that we are working together as a team. And as a team, we're heading toward common goals to get positive results.

When you think of confrontation, you shouldn't cringe.

Behavior-focused

Always focus on the behavior, not the person! When you confront Terry, it's not like a law officer saying, "Terry, you're a bad driver. You get a ticket." It's saying, as a coach, "Terry, we have a problem. I'm going to work with you to help improve performance in this (specific) area. We're going to work it through because we want to get the best results." The idea is to help the team member perform. A counselor improves nothing by saying, "I can't believe you blew it again." As a StaffCoach™, you exist to build up, not tear down. *Behavior should be your first focus ... not the person!*

Opportunity-focused

It's common to view confrontation not as a tool to build the best performance possible, but as criticism. But there's a difference between confrontation and criticism. Confrontation deals with issues of missed *opportunity* ... specifically as it affects the team's ability to succeed. Criticism, on the other hand, usually deals with the individual's attitude. Criticism focuses on flaws within the person rather than on opportunities for achievement that are available through altered behavior.

Specific

Confrontation is very *specific*. Criticism tends to be more general and is frequently couched in blame or fault. When we criticize we tend to use generalities — words and phrases like *always, never, everybody, all the time.*

Listed on the next page are 10 negative (critical) remarks a manager might be tempted to make when confronting a team member about his performance. To the right are spaces for you to rewrite each phrase into a positive confrontational expression. When writing your remarks, ask yourself: Would this make me angry if someone said it to me? Does this remark close or open doors to effective communication? Does the team member have an opportunity to respond without incriminating himself?

> *As a StaffCoach™, you exist to build up, not tear down.*

Critical remark

Didn't you hear me tell
you not to do that?

I can't believe you
actually did that!

Why are these things
always happening to you?

Nobody else ever has
those problems.

What will it take to
make you understand?

If this doesn't stop, we're going
to have a real problem.

How can I give you a
raise when these
kinds of things happen?

I've really had it with you.

If you can't get a handle on
this, we'll have to find
someone who can.

Why can't you do it the
way Bob does?

Positive remark

Was there something about
my directions that might have
been unclear?

Let's look at what happened
and try to figure out what
went wrong.

_____

_____

_____

_____

_____

_____

_____

_____

E
X
E
R
C
I
S
E

Cooperative

There is a significant but often misunderstood difference between confrontation and criticism. Confrontation, when done appropriately, builds cooperation, while criticism, even when it's intended to be constructive, usually leaves the other party feeling attacked or at least less than adequate. The ability to confront an individual hinges on separating the person from the problem, confronting the problem while paying attention to the individual. For example: "Jim, I understand you have a great deal of time in this project. I'd like to work with you to make sure we don't slip further off track on the deadlines."

Confrontation sends the message, "I'm concerned about this, as I'm sure you are; let's work on this together." Criticism, on the other hand, is a direct negative opinion delivered with little regard for the person. For example: "This is a major problem; what are you doing about it?"

Although motives and intention can easily become blurred, especially during heated conversations over things we care about, the important thing is to ensure cooperation when everything is said and done. Without cooperation, you'll be left doing it yourself, or things won't get done at all.

Encouraging

In short, confrontation should be a specialized form of *encouraging* — a positive experience. Criticism is almost always viewed (especially by the person who receives it) as a negative action. Sure, some behaviors need to change — but change can and should be an encouraging prospect ... not a discouraging one.

THE FIVE-STEP CONFRONTATION PROCESS

A positive attitude is especially important when you need to confront a problem employee. As we discussed earlier, the purpose of confronting is to correct and help the person behave in a more acceptable manner. It is positive — not negative — and never harsh! Confrontation may never be the most pleasant thing in the world for you to do, but you can make it a lot easier — and less emotional — by applying a *five-step confrontation technique* to your sessions.

- **Be honest**
- **Take the initiative**
- **Time the confrontation well**
- **Mean what you say**
- **Be human**

1. Be honest

Don't beat around the bush. You're not doing anyone any favors if you distort the truth to save feelings. Sure, you should be conscious of feelings, but not *immobilized* by them. The temptation to talk about anything else (the weather, the economy, "those Bears," etc.) except the uncomfortable situation in question may be strong. But don't yield to it. Hesitancy to come straight at the issue now may make the employee think you're not serious about the problem. Be pleasant but be persistent.

2. Take the initiative

Actively address the reason for meeting with the person. Work toward resolving the problem ... together ... in specific ways. Some counselors find that filling out the following worksheet (or something like it) during the discussion helps. But don't look like you're filling out a grade card! Give the employee a clear view of the form ... even give him a copy to fill out with you, if you feel that might help keep your discussion mutually focused and controlled.

> *When the great help the small, both are just the right size.*

> *Be pleasant but be persistent.*

165

PROBLEM-SOLVING DISCUSSION AID

1. The problem attitude or behavior is _____
   _____

2. What makes it a problem?
   To the team _____
   To the individual_____
   To the organization_____

3. What circumstances contributed to the problem?
   _____
   _____

4. List three ways you might keep the circumstances from happening again:
   _____
   _____
   _____

5. Action(s) to be taken to correct the behavior:
   _____
   _____

6. Consequences of unacceptable behavior:
   _____
   _____

7. Consequences of correct behavior:
   _____
   _____

Remember, problem behavior is like a bruise. Press in the center and ... ouch! No fun. Press on the outside edges and the pain is much less. But any coach will tell you that a bruise doesn't get well until its center is dispersed by heat or massage therapy. What's the moral? The problem won't go away until you deal directly with it. Don't dance around the edges.

3. Time the confrontation well

If the problem is a recurring one, try to confront the person as soon as possible after the problem behavior has occurred. However, if the behavior has made you angry or upset, delay confrontation. Initiate confrontation only when you have control of your emotions, or the only problem that will be noticed is your lack of emotional control.

4. Mean what you say

Don't say anything you're not prepared to back up. If you resolve to say only what you can enforce, you'll probably show little or no anger in your voice or expression. Anyone who has ever heard a parent lose control understands that anger creates unrealistic demands ... and it makes claims you cannot stand behind.

Example:

"Jimmy, I want you home faster than you can say 'jack rabbit'!"

(How realistic is *that*, Mom?)

"Betsy, if you don't stop fidgeting and talking, I'm never taking you to a movie again."

(So, the child's last movie in life is "Snow White"? C'mon, Dad!)

The moral? Be cool and you'll be in control — which usually means you'll be communicating!

Be cool and you'll be in control.

5. Be human

Don't carry unnecessary baggage into the confrontation about how you must look or act as a counselor. Be yourself. That may mean your mouth doesn't feel like it's working right, or your left eye twitches, or your voice cracks. Big deal. You're there to help your team and struggling team member, not to look perfect. And when the session is over ... even when the tone or the outcome was not especially great ... let the team member know you still value him as a person.

"Thanks for your time, Rhea. Are you and Ken going to the company picnic?"

"Thanks for coming, Phil. Now let's go see how many mountains of new work have sprung up on our desks since we've been gone!"

Remember: "Firm" is human. "Forgiving" is human. Hard and unfeeling are not.

Learning to confront team members about performance issues as a counselor is one link in the chain of "connective interaction" between the StaffCoach™ and team member(s). Another link is working together to change the substandard behavior. One formula for that is to answer the following eight revealing questions. Your answers should be very enlightening ... very educational.

EIGHT WAYS TO ELIMINATE UNSATISFACTORY BEHAVIOR

1. What are the actual facts of the situation?

Don't trust your emotional recollection of the *effects* of the behavior — what *exactly* has been or is being done improperly? List the offense(s) objectively. If you're in doubt about what happened, seek out confidential, firsthand observers. Never list what you think: List what you know.

> *"My players need me more when they lose than when they win."*
>
> *— Jim Valvano*

168

For instance, don't settle for being told something like, "Ann was late twice last week in the middle of our busiest selling season." Dig a little deeper. You might discover that Ann arrived four minutes late on Thursday and eight minutes late on Friday, but she worked through her lunch hour both days.

2. What is the specific behavior you want changed?

Remember, we aren't discussing attitude. That's not behavior. If it *is* an attitude problem, talking about the specific behavior could reveal it and address it. For instance, addressing poor performance (behavior) by Frank could reveal his resentment (attitude) over what he considers unfair work assignments. Explaining assignment rationale and sharing its long-term benefits for the whole team could help restore acceptable performance levels.

Here again, be specific about the behavior you want changed. Is changing the behavior a one-step process, or might it require many steps over a period of time? Will Frank need short-term productivity goals that you and he review weekly? Will he need outside training on the processes or equipment critical to his job? Think it through!

3. What open-ended question(s) could create dialogue?

"Terry, we have a problem with your decision to (name the behavior). How do you see us resolving it together?" Or, "What steps might we take to make it easier to (state the correct behavior) in the future?" These are open-ended questions. As you'll learn on the next page, open-ended questions don't put people on the defensive. They help put both parties on a healing offensive by encouraging dialogue — because they demand more than a "yes" or "no" response.

Attitude is not behavior.

Examples:

CLOSED-ENDED (CHALLENGING) QUESTIONS	OPEN-ENDED (INVITING) QUESTIONS
Are you responsible for this error?	What can you tell me about this problem?
Will this step solve the problem?	What can we do to make sure this will solve the problem?
Do you understand what you're supposed to do?	Is there anything about the job that might still be a little unclear?
Are you going to meet the deadline?	What steps would help you meet the deadline?
Have you finished the Acme job?	Where are you on the Acme project?

4. How can you establish the need for change?

To establish a need for change, the counselor should show how the specific behavior affects three areas:

- The individual
- The group
- The organization

Consequences stated in this way etch the full impact of the behavior in the team member's mind — and puts the focus on the problem instead of the individual.

Put the focus on the problem instead of the individual.

Example:

Mike:
I should have finished this manuscript a long time ago, Ellen. You've been more than patient. I'm sure I can finish it soon now.

Ellen/Coach:
Can you give me an idea how soon that might be?

Mike:
Well ... I have to fit in some other account demand, unfortunately, so ... I'd say three weeks. Maybe four.

Ellen:
If I give you five weeks, would you feel comfortable about committing to a final deadline?

Mike:
I can't imagine why not.

Ellen:
Good. Because after that date, the department release schedule would be badly affected — which means the entire organizational publication projection would be thrown off.

Mike:
Makes the script sound pretty crucial.

Ellen:
Right. Missing this deadline would do more than affect your chances for future scripts. It could hurt the company's bottom line.

Mike:
Then I'd better get busy. Thanks for giving me the whole picture, Ellen.

> *The smallest accomplishment is better than the grandest intention.*

5. Who has been assigned responsibility for the problem?

Who is responsible directly? Indirectly? Include yourself in the latter category, because it's not just the team member's problem. It's your problem, too — not just because of organizational policy, but because you have team standards that won't be compromised.

Many managers tend to place the *real* concern about the employee's problems or substandard behavior "up the ladder." They make it seem as if company standards are strictly a top-down issue. That tendency shows itself in remarks like, "*They* will come down hard on me if this continues ... " or "*The company* expects you to change because ... ." Such an approach may seem to free the counselor from being the "bad guy" in a confrontation — but it creates three deadly long-term problems:

- The employee receives the implied message that you wouldn't object to the behavior if you were in a position to set a *more reasonable* policy.

- The behavior will only become less obvious ... hidden from the *unreasonable* policy-setters above ... but won't be gone altogether.

- You'll find it almost impossible to expect compliance from that employee when it comes to future direction, because you look powerless. Make sure he understands that you own the issues and problems.

6. How will you help to achieve change?

Answering this one must always mean a time commitment. Change happens over time. Will change mean returning to mentoring in some areas? Will it mean involving "referral" agents to more thoroughly equip the team member? Prepare in advance your commitment alternatives, and remember: No change is possible without a time investment.

Change happens over time.

7. What are the minimum standards you will accept?

Decide in advance what standards are non-negotiable and define them during the counseling session. Such non-negotiables (attendance, procedures, work output, relational activities, etc.) should be in writing ... specific and measurable. If you don't have those formalized guidelines, you'll find yourself in "agreement" trouble. Know what your minimums are and why — and at least three ways your team member can accomplish those minimums.

Examples:

> **Standard:** 40 hours per workweek
> **Compliance options/opportunities:**
> > **a.** 9 a.m. to 5 p.m., Monday through Friday
> > **b.** 8 a.m. to 2:45 p.m., Monday through Saturday
> > **c.** 8 a.m. to 6 p.m., Monday through Thursday
>
> **Standard:** Meet weekly production schedules
> **Compliance options/opportunities:**
> > **a.** Set daily goals
> > **b.** Review progress and problems with group leader every evening
> > **c.** Hire temporary help, when needed, using money from year-end bonus fund
>
> **Standard:** Be at work on time
> **Compliance options/opportunities:**
> > **a.** Buy new alarm clock or ask co-worker for wake-up call
> > **b.** Go to bed earlier and/or leave for work earlier
> > **c.** Join a department car pool

8. What rewards can and will you give?

Remember, rewards aren't bribes. They are not carrots managers must dangle in front of team members before they can expect decent performance. Rewards are important aspects of performance management, however. We all expect positive consequences for positive effort — and they doesn't necessarily have to involve money.

Rewards aren't bribes.

173

Here are a few examples of the happy little "extras" that will communicate (1) your appreciation for positive change in employee performance and (2) your intention to respond positively to such accomplishment in the future.

Rewards:

- Use of the company tickets to a sporting event
- Gift certificate to dinner and/or a movie
- Written or verbal acknowledgment in the presence of peers and/or superiors
- Personal time off
- Extended lunch or break time(s)
- Work-related gift (pen, pocket calendar, desk plant, etc.)
- Special outside training events
- Promotion
- Bonus or salary increase

The more valuable the ground, the more necessary the plowing.

COUNSELING EVALUATION EXERCISE

Now think of a team member who consistently delivers
unsatisfactory behavior. That may mean coming to work late,
goofing off or failing to complete work properly. Answer these
eight questions about the last time you counseled him.

1. **Did I take the time to know all the facts?**

2. **Did I explain the specific behavior I wanted to change?**

3. **Were my questions closed-ended or open-ended?**

4. **Did I communicate the reasons the change was required?**

5. **Did I include myself in the problem?**

6. **How did I provide opportunities for change?**

7. **What minimum standards did I communicate?**

8. **Did I offer positive consequences when change occurs?**

If you have thought through these questions and listed your
answers, you will have developed an abbreviated action plan
for dealing with any difficult behavior.

10 FREEING ESSENTIALS OF FACE-TO-FACE COUNSELING

Let's deal now with some basic techniques that defuse the potential for explosive counseling sessions. You've learned the philosophy of confrontation and the key questions you should answer to improve substandard behavior. Now let's look at the pressure-reducing steps you can take to hold a positive, productive counseling session.

- **Maintain privacy.**
- **Avoid referring to third parties.**
- **Minimize interruptions.**
- **Avoid distractions.**
- **Plan ahead and finish on time.**
- **Control your emotions in advance.**
- **Establish the facts.**
- **Assess probable impact.**
- **Seek behavior-related change.**
- **Determine minimum performance standards.**

1. Maintain privacy.

This simple rule will guarantee confidentiality and, ultimately, trust. Make sure your meeting takes place where doors can be closed. Assure the team member that your discussion is between you and him. Ask for that same commitment from your employee.

> *Maintaining privacy will guarantee confidentiality.*

2. Avoid referring to third parties as much as possible.

Example: "You know, so and so said this, so I thought it was time we talked." Third-party references are very risky. They imply that you have accepted hearsay before consulting with the team member who is the object of the information. But the bottom line is that third-party references (even if valid) usually succeed only in producing defensiveness.

3. Make sure no interruptions will occur.

Have you ever been in someone's office and the person's phone keeps ringing and interrupting you? What does that communicate? Simple: You're not important. Here's what a good counselor must do: When someone comes to your office, notify whoever is handling visitors and incoming calls that you are indisposed until a specific time. If you think you might be interrupted by an upper-management emergency, tell the team member about that possibility — and apologize in advance. When employees hear that, they know you believe they are important.

4. Avoid distractions.

When you conduct a face-to-face meeting, choose an environment that won't distract you. Offices with no windows are best for this — especially if the windows open onto another office environment.

5. Plan ahead and finish on time.

Have you ever been told, "I need five minutes of your time," and it cost you an hour? Frustrating, isn't it? You can avoid that by making a meeting agenda. It doesn't have to be a detailed, multi-page affair — just a short outline will do. But it will keep you on time and on target, while giving your team member a sense of what you want to cover and how far along you are in the meeting.

6. Gain control of your emotions before you start.

How will you make sure your emotions are under control? Many managers recommend two ways: (a) Make your breathing regular and deep, and (b) guard your tone of voice.

One effective way to chase emotion from your voice is to talk more slowly. Concentrate on speaking each word precisely and rather softly. Amazingly, if you get your voice tone under control, your emotions invariably follow!

If you get your voice tone under control, your emotions invariably follow!

"Broad brush" words like always, never, all the time and everybody only antagonize.

7. Establish the facts with specific details.

We discussed this earlier. Don't speak in generalities. "Broad brush" words like *always, never, all the time* and *everybody* only antagonize. Make a three or five-point description of the specific facts before the meeting — then stick to it.

8. Assess the probable impact on your team member.

What reactions can you reasonably expect during your counseling session? How has the team member reacted to these kinds of exchanges in the past? What is happening in his life that might amplify or alter a "normal" response? Anticipating the team member's reactions will be valuable preparation for your session. For instance, what if you have reason to believe that Kristen's response to your counseling session might be very emotional? She may even start crying or yelling and run from your office. How can you prepare for such a possibility?

    a. Document your planned session and state your concern about Kristen's possible response to your supervisor and/or your human resources director. One or both of them might have valuable suggestions for handling the session.

    b. Identify the part of the meeting that is most likely to upset Kristen and "defuse" it as much as possible. If Kristen's poor performance is jeopardizing team productivity as well as her job, practice different ways to communicate that fact accurately but sensitively.

        WRONG:
        "Kristen, we can't keep you on if things don't improve."

        POSSIBLE:
        "Kristen, have you thought of anything that might be preventing your ability to improve since we talked last?"

        POSSIBLE:
        "Kristen, if you had to name two or three things that keep you from performing as well as you want to, what would they be?"

c. Don't counsel Kristen alone. She should be aware that a third person will be nearby — perhaps just outside your meeting place. Having this person in the room would not promote the confidential environment most counseling sessions benefit from, but his presence could provide a supportive account of any incidents you anticipate.

9. Make sure the changes are behavior-related.

As we've already discussed, the desired changes should be aimed at behavior, not attitude. That's the only real change you can make in someone — and the only change that ultimately alters attitude.

10. Determine your minimum standard of performance.

You must have a measuring stick. You must know what you should reasonably want. The team member can help determine how to rise to that standard, but you alone must define what the standard is.

> *The only real change you can make in someone is in behavior, not attitude.*

CASE STUDY

CASE STUDY

Reed Thurman was shipping manager for Ramco Roofing
Co. His team included a secretary, a dispatch clerk, a dock
foreman, a warehouse supervisor, three fork-lift drivers
and eight dock hands. Reed reported to the owner of the
company, Lester Sisk. Reed's dock foreman, Chester Brook,
was a veteran overseer. Chester's crew was divided into
two teams that he changed every two or three months.
The teams held monthly contests that were won or lost
based on the speed, neatness and accuracy with which
trucks were loaded at the dock as orders were received
and filled.

Over the last few months, Reed's dispatch clerk had
reported an increase in client complaints that orders had
arrived with a high percentage of improper roofing
materials. The problem had finally come to Mr. Sisk's
attention. He held a closed-door session with Reed
ordering him to make sure the trend stopped ... or else!

Reed immediately called Chester in and angrily told him to
stop the team truck-loading contests. "Your guys are
getting more concerned with winning a case of beer than
with getting the right stuff to the customer."

Chester was stunned. "These are the best guys I've ever
supervised! Even when they're moving fast, they load
things neat and right and ..."

" ... and wrong!" Reed interrupted. "No more contests,
Ches. End of discussion!"

During the next three months, client complaints all but
disappeared. Mr. Sisk was pleased. But dock-crew
resignations resulted in six new employees. Among those
who quit was Chester Brook. One afternoon, Reed
Thurman's new dock foreman asked if he could change
the way shipping invoices were checked on the dock.

"Why?" Reed asked him. "It's always worked OK before."

"Well," the new foreman observed, "the current way of

checking a pallet of material as it leaves the warehouse could allow a forklift driver to load it on the wrong truck — especially when we are moving fast. We really should be checking material as it enters the truck."

Reed swallowed hard. "What made you think of that?" he asked.

"Oh, some of these young replacements we've hired were seeing who could load a truck faster and I noticed one of their forklift drivers putting a pallet on the wrong truck," the foreman answered. "By the way," he added, "if it's OK with you, I was thinking about having regular monthly contests like that to sort of build up morale. Would you have any problem with that?"

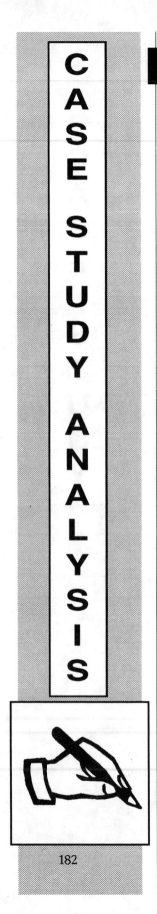

C
A
S
E

S
T
U
D
Y

A
N
A
L
Y
S
I
S

CASE STUDY ANALYSIS

1. Which of the 10 essentials of face-to-face counseling did Reed Thurman use?

2. Which did he violate?

3. Which did not really apply?

4. Which one of the 10 essentials could have uncovered the real problem and avoided the employee turnover?

5. What part did Reed's emotions play in this unfortunate scenario?

6. What third party influenced Reed's judgment? Why?

7. What one lesson from this case study can help you most in future counseling sessions?

FIVE STEPS TO MODIFYING BEHAVIOR

"Behavior modification" became a big phrase during the '70s and '80s. And it should *still* be a big phrase in the offices of organizational counselors everywhere. Why? Because modifying behavior perfectly describes what a team does in order to win. And since you coach a team that wants to avoid defeat, modifying behavior has to be at the top of your "must do" list.

Here are five approaches to modifying behavior ... yours and your employees' ... that will produce dramatic victories if practiced faithfully:

- **Gain agreement about the problem.**
- **Agree on necessary action.**
- **Identify consequences.**
- **Tie consequences to basic needs.**
- **Reward achievement.**

1. Gain agreement that a problem exists.

The very first thing that must happen in any counseling session is to sit down with the person concerned and agree "we've" got a problem. That may not be as easy as it sounds — but without it, the rest of behavior modification doesn't mean anything. If you can't get agreement that a problem exists, a resolution is impossible. Your first goal, therefore, is to gain that agreement. Remember, it helps considerably to discuss the problem as "our" problem, not as just the team member's problem.

2. Mutually agree on the action to be taken.

This requires employee participation in the improvement process. One way to help ensure this is to ask the employee how he thinks the problem might be solved. Chances are, at least some aspect of the team member's solution can become part of a plan you've already thought through. Results? The team member has some ownership in the solution and a greater commitment to get things done.

Discuss the problem as "our" problem, not just the team member's problem.

3. Identify the consequences of action and inaction.

This point is a must in any improvement process. Not only should you not side-step it, you should ideally formalize agreement on consequences by asking, "Do we have an agreement on expectations and consequences?"

Some managers like to document the counseling session and ask for signature affirmation from the team member concerning expectations and consequences. The approach you take will vary with the organization and your own style. But the important thing to remember is to end every counseling session by recapping decisions and focusing on action to be taken. Talking about substandard behavior is good. But behavior that isn't targeted for specific action will never change.

And, of course, consequences must be specific: "If we can't see at least a 5-percent increase by this time next month, Roy, I feel we must (consequences). Does that seem right to you?" You may need to plan ahead to figure out what consequences are right for the needs of the employee in question. It's probably not something you can do on the spot. And remember, the counseling session should cover positive as well as negative consequences. Focusing only on the negative will communicate expectations of failure. Point to the benefits of following through on the proper behavior you have targeted.

4. Make sure the consequences affect basic needs.

If you don't tie the consequences of poor performance to basic needs, the employee will continue to perform unsatisfactorily.

Consequences must be specific.

Examples:

Consequence (Negative)	Basic Employee Need
Closer supervision	Increasing independence
No promotion	Growth and affirmation
Reduced responsibilities	Pride in achievement
Reduced income	Consistent lifestyle

Consequence (Positive)	Basic Employee Need
Team interaction	Belonging, involvement
Flex time	Autonomy and personal control
Cross training	Growth and development

No consequences will motivate any two people exactly the same way — but *motivating consequences can be found for any team member.* Just remember: Human beings change negative behavior only when consequences encourage ... even *force* ... positive behavior.

5. Reward achievement.

Changing any negative behavior permanently demands external motivation. And, as we've discussed, the best motivation isn't always money. For instance, showing that new behavior will benefit the employee's health, safety or status (through promotion, etc.) often provides the needed incentive to change behavior.

The best motivation isn't always money.

BEHAVIOR MODIFICATION EXERCISE

Now, to sharpen your confrontation skills, try writing a scenario of your own. Pick a problem team member (past, present or imaginary) and write how you think you could induce that person to respond positively to a confrontation through your use of the five approaches just discussed.

Employee name:_____

Substandard behavior:_____

IN COUNSELING THIS PERSON, HOW WOULD YOU ...

1. Gain agreement about the problem?

2. Agree on necessary action?

3. Identify consequences?

4. Tie consequences to basic needs?

5. Reward achievement?

HOW TO ASK QUESTIONS THAT GET THE ANSWERS YOU NEED

Have you ever tried to communicate with someone who continually gives one-word answers ("yep" or "nope") to your questions? Maybe you aren't asking the right questions — and, as mentioned earlier, the right questions can be critical to understanding what motivates, troubles, inspires, angers or 'impresses team members. The right questions create dialogue. How? By being "open-ended."

As we discussed earlier in this chapter, open-ended questions are a lost art in most work environments. Instead, managers give commands. Things like, "Tell me." "Explain to me." When you substitute commands for questions, people automatically become defensive ... and dialogue shuts down.

Open-ended questions create rapport. They don't demand a yes or no answer. They're easy to identify because they usually start with one of these words: Who, What, Where, When, How or Why.

Open-ended questions accomplish five key objectives. They:

1. Minimize defensive responses

2. Show the speaker's interest in the listener's ideas

3. Communicate an openness — freedom from "right" or "wrong" answers

4. Are 100 percent more likely to stimulate conversation

5. Create a sense of "team" ... of pulling together toward mutual victory

The right questions create dialogue.

EXERCISE: CREATING OPEN-ENDED ALTERNATIVES

On page 170, we looked at examples of closed-ended questions and at the open-ended alternatives that would encourage things like dialogue and mutual respect. Now it's your turn to provide the alternatives. Rewrite each of the questions shown here into questions that accomplish one or more of the five objectives just discussed.

CLOSED-ENDED QUESTIONS	OPEN-ENDED ALTERNATIVES
How long are we going to have to put up with this kind of behavior from you?	_____ _____
What in the world made you do such a dumb thing?	_____ _____
Is this the best you can do?	_____
Didn't I ask you not to do it that way?	_____ _____
Everyone else has to suffer because of your mistakes.	_____ _____
If you can't get this right, how can I trust you with more responsibility?	_____ _____
You are becoming known as a problem.	_____ _____

The ability to ask open-ended questions is vital to your success as a counselor. Take every opportunity to ask them because they let you tap into the unlimited resources of the people who work for you.

RECOGNIZING THE RESULTS OF COUNSELING THAT WORKS

If you are an effective counselor, what kind of results can you expect to see? Here are five of the most obvious benefits:

1. Shared ownership of goals

Team members ... maybe for the first time ... will begin to understand how performance goals relate to them individually and how to achieve those goals.

2. New errors don't become old errors

Your team members will develop an awareness of what constitutes good and bad work, and will be more inclined to: (1) want to please you, (2) increase team productivity and (3) halt negative behavior before it becomes habitual.

3. Employees become teammates

Successful counseling promotes the importance of individuals contributing to the whole. Counseling reduces the individual's sense of being a "lone ranger," whether performing poorly or well. All behavior affects the team and the team members know it.

4. Strong goal orientation

Counselors who experience the greatest success have helped team members leap roadblocks by setting and achieving meaningful short- and long-term goals. They teach *the power of goal-setting*. What's that? Perhaps this power is best illustrated by recalling the old riddle: "How do you eat an elephant?" The answer: "One bite at a time."

Always work with the construction gang and not the wrecking crew.

Good counselors acknowledge the long-term goal (eating the elephant), but they focus on the short-term measures (one bite at a time) that make the final vision achievable. Once the team experiences the power of goal-setting, it becomes a familiar, trustworthy team tool.

5. Confrontations are fewer...and increasingly positive

Isn't this every manager's dream? The good news is it doesn't have to be a dream. Implementing the confrontation principles outlined in this chapter can make fewer confrontations a reality!

"Action may not always bring success, but there is no success without it."

— Benjamin Disraeli

EXERCISE: IS COUNSELING WORKING FOR YOUR TEAM?

Under each of the points listed below (and discussed previously) note (1) the positive results of counseling evident in your team environment, (2) any results your team may lack, and (3) specific steps you could take to experience improvement.

BENEFITS OF COUNSELING	TRUE/FALSE	EXPLAIN	ACTION TO IMPROVE
1. Shared ownership of goals			
2. New errors don't become old errors			
3. Employees become teammates			
4. Strong goal orientation			
5. Confrontations are fewer and increasingly positive			

After reading this chapter, if your view of the counseling role is one of promoter rather than police officer ... of healer rather than henchman ... of director rather than dictator ... you've got the right idea. A counselor isn't someone who pushes "square" team members into "round" organizational holes. He helps team members discover how their own talents and types ... as well as the organization's needs and objectives ... can be tailored to a custom fit.

The counselor's task is to mold and shape. That process means helping people stretch ... helping people develop flexibility ... helping people allow themselves and their futures to be creatively shaped permanently.

When you start to see your counseling role as one of molding lives and start to take pleasure in it, your team members will be in capable hands!

A counselor doesn't push "square" team members into "round" organizational holes.

CHAPTER QUIZ

1. What are the four keys to effective counseling?

2. Name three of the five steps to positive confrontation.

3. List eight ways to eliminate unsatisfactory behavior.

4. Name five of the 10 elements of productive counseling sessions.

5. Who is one team member you look forward to "molding" over the next few months?

CHAPTER 6

The High-Performance Team

"One of the hardest skills for a manager to learn is how to build a team. One of the hardest skills for a manager to teach is how to be a member of a team."
— *Randall Wright*

INSTILLING TEAM VISION

The greatest thrill of successful StaffCoaching™ is building a team that works together for inspired performance. Given the right vision and guidance, any team can achieve new levels of performance. In a visionary environment of trust and commitment, people develop strengths they never knew they had.

Every truly great coach in history had a vision ... a dream of what a team could achieve. And great coaches communicate that vision to their teams in a way that inspires.

If you want to be an outstanding StaffCoach™ and to build a team that achieves inspired performance, you need to have a vision, and then you need to share it. You must make every person on your team feel that she has a personal stake in the

Randall Wright has owned, started up from scratch and turned around a number of businesses — all of which have been high-contact customer service ventures. ("The hardest way and the easiest way to make a buck. Nothing is harder than super customer service and so few do it well, that when you do people flock to you.") He graduated from the University of Kansas with a bachelor's degree in pharmacy. His communication talents have also given him the opportunity to be involved in many projects, including as talk show host for a major market radio station and newspaper columnist for several highly respected dailies and weeklies.

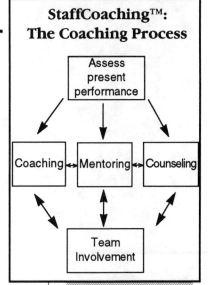

StaffCoaching™: The Coaching Process

Assess present performance

Coaching ↔ Mentoring ↔ Counseling

Team Involvement

Only with vision can you have a winning team.

vision. You must give your people a vision that meets their needs and motivates them to be the best they can be.

Without a vision, the team is just a work group ... a "unit," with each person doing her job ... just getting through the day. Only with vision can you have a winning team. Do you have a vision for your team?

Here's how you can:

1. Write out your highest hopes ...

... your most ambitious expectations ... your most cherished dreams for your team. Don't limit yourself at this stage. Involve the whole team. Shoot for the moon. Then, even if you miss, at least you'll end up in the stars, right? Make your vision one that will inspire people and assure them they are working for something great!

Examples:

- To operate as a totally self-directed team within the next 18 months

- To enroll every member of the team in at least two job-related educational experiences every year

- To achieve and sustain the highest level of productivity in company history

- To have a 100 percent accident-free work record for one full year

- To operate for 90 days without receiving one customer complaint about department service.

2. Link your vision to organizational goals.

How does your vision line up with the corporate direction ... with your market ... with your budget? If you create a vision that's out of sync with these key business elements, you and your team are setting yourselves up for frustration.

Let's say one of your department goals is to increase product quantity, but the driving division goal is to increase quality. You could be in the unenviable position of receiving team reprimands even when your team members exceed your goals! Always make sure your "mission" or "vision" is based on and complements the larger corporate objective.

3. Develop a strategic path for reaching your vision.

Identify the necessary steps and resources you need. Identify the tools your team will need to work effectively toward achieving your vision. For instance, if your goal is to increase sales by 20 percent during the third quarter, list the specific "behaviors" that will accomplish that, such as: Make 10 more calls per day ... Attend "How to Sell Effectively" seminar ... Develop new leads from old customer referrals. Where do these "behaviors" come from? From your team. Brainstorming sessions with your team to develop action steps not only create a stronger sense of unified purpose but also give each member ownership in the resulting plan.

Once you've listed the steps to your goals, ask your boss to review your written recommendations. Get her ideas ... and approval.

4. Implement your vision.

Once you have input from team members and approval from your leadership, transfer the "ownership" of the strategic plan to your people. Then get out of their way! Sure, you should show your willingness to provide ongoing, positive and constructive feedback — and, when it's time, to provide direction and support. But your team must know that you endorse reasonable risk-taking and that failure isn't terminal as long as productive learning results from it.

> *Brainstorming sessions create a stronger sense of unified purpose.*

RECOGNIZING THE POTENTIAL FOR TEAM TROUBLE

To keep your team running smoothly, you must stay alert to signs of trouble. If you know the most common warning signals, you can usually block major problems.

Here are six common signals employees may send that say they are losing momentum on the job.

1. They are falling behind.

When job progress slows down because team members can't seem to get their work done on time, check your lines of communication! Either (a) you aren't inspiring and motivating through regular team meetings, (b) your leaders aren't telling you about specific productivity or workflow stumbling blocks or (c) general unspoken resentment exists among team members. Roll up your sleeves and get to work. Communication starts with you!

2. Team-member actions or plans are vague.

Employees have difficulty explaining how specific jobs will be accomplished. Stop the presses! Don't move another inch until these uncertainties are dealt with — whether through team brainstorming sessions, new job or project descriptions, or clarified expectations for procedures and deadlines.

Coach:
Well, this looks good, Barb. I think you should probably go with it — but how will you hand off to shipping when Don has his job finished? That looks kind of critical.

Barb:
It really shouldn't be any problem. Don has had that part of the project under control for a long time.

Coach:
You're probably right. But you've got a couple of new wrinkles that might confuse him. It sure would me. Does he know about them?

When job progress slows down, check your lines of communication.

Barb:
Well, generally.

Coach:
You should get specific with him. I wouldn't want you to get all the way to Don's department before discovering a glitch. Other than that, let's do it. Great job!

3. Employees become overly optimistic about projects.

This is difficult to detect, especially because optimistic enthusiasm is exactly what we like to hear. But watch out! Team members may bite off more than they can chew in the interest of pleasing you or making the team look good. The danger is that unrealistic optimism sets up your team for failure — maybe even repeated failure. Make sure someone objectively monitors project goals, and make sure your people know they don't have to be super-humans to be superstars on your team!

4. Increase in employee anger or stress is noticeable.

Reasons for irritated team members can be many and varied, but you can usually identify them through counseling. You may discover a well-concealed dispute between two or more members that has team-crippling side effects.

Maybe general dissent exists over a new policy or procedure. Ask questions — and ask as many team members as it takes until a consensus begins to surface. Is there a grievance, condition, event or personality that runs like a thread through each counseling interview? Does Joe's name surface repeatedly in a negative way? Does the plan to relocate the department to another floor keep coming up? Or the company-wide salary cut? The starting point for uncovering widespread dissension is talking to your team.

> *Team members may bite off more than they can chew to please you or to make the team look good.*

5. Absenteeism increases.

Absenteeism is also a strong signal that something is wrong. As in No. 4, getting involved with your people and pinpointing likely causes of the problem are critical to finding solutions. In the meantime, consequences for absenteeism should be reviewed. If absenteeism is widespread, consequences apparently aren't strong enough.

6. Employees avoid contact and/or conversation.

When one of your team members starts avoiding you, the reasons can be many. Among them might be:

- General unease in the presence of authority

- Performance anxiety — fear of communicating in a way that isn't "good" or adequate

- Fear of being asked to do something

- Dread of being asked what she has done about a specific task

- Guilt over real or imagined poor *performance*

The remedy for all these has its roots in coach "contact" — constant, consistent contact. The more time you spend with team members, the more they view you as being genuinely interested in promoting individual success — and the fewer the negative incidents will be. As you become human and accessible, your team will become open and free of distrust.

When the entire team seems to avoid you, however, the probable causes can be quite different.

- A problem exists and your anticipated solution is not what they want to hear.

- A decision, assignment, attitude or action of yours (real or rumored) has communicated an anti-team message.

Absenteeism is a strong signal that something is wrong.

- An unpopular procedure or policy "from the top" has made you guilty by association.

You can respond to these team problems in one of three basic ways:

- *Do nothing* — wait until someone shares the problem, then address it. This approach works best when you are virtually positive the problem involves something you can't change — such as a company-wide policy about shorter lunch hours. In time, such unrest almost always diminishes and even disappears. Confronting the unrest before it runs its course can fuel fires that would have otherwise extinguished themselves.

- *Meet with key team members*, individually or together. Ask what's going on and why. List the facts and (now or later) deal with each one at a time, asking for input and ideas. When these key members are satisfied that either (1) you are aware of the problem and are taking steps to work with them to resolve it or (2) your joint solution is acceptable, then they can give the results of your meeting to the other team members.

- *Call a team meeting*. Clear the air. Invite honest, open discussion about any problems that team members may see as unresolved. Your willingness to meet issues head-on will be more important than your ability to "fix" things on the spot. Just listen. Take notes. Let people talk. Discuss solution options ... even assign "solution teams" if possible.

In every instance, with an individual or a group, the key to dealing positively with defensiveness or aloofness is the same: Face the problem at the first opportunity. When your team members see you want positive, constructive confrontation, they will increasingly tend to speak their concerns ... and be less and less likely to hide them.

Face the problem at the first opportunity.

CASE STUDY

Linda Benchley's team of computer technicians worked with some of the most expensive inventory at MacMasters Inc. Eighteen full-time technicians formed the nucleus of the MacMasters service department. They were divided into three teams of six members each, with each member specializing in different Macintosh computer models and hardware configurations.

When one of the teams began missing expensive parts, Linda and the team leader met to discuss the problem. The team leader, Rob, reluctantly admitted that he suspected one of his people of theft. Linda and Rob carefully documented their information before meeting with Becky, the team member Rob suspected.

Becky was well liked by every employee and was a favorite with regular MacMasters customers. Her special talents with computer repairs as well as her quick sense of humor made everyone appreciate her. Becky's brother, Mark, was also a technician in the service department. When Becky was told about the disappearance of parts from her area, she hotly denied any wrongdoing. Linda carefully explained that no one was being accused — only questioned for information.

During the next six months, more parts disappeared. When questioned again, Becky claimed to know nothing about the disappearance. Then finally Rob saw her slip a new memory board into her briefcase before leaving work one day. When Becky was dismissed three days later, she returned the parts or the dollar equivalent of everything she had taken in order to avoid prosecution. Out of deference to Becky's brother, Mark, and out of concern that customers might hesitate to trust their hardware to MacMasters technicians, the company did not tell service department personnel why Becky was dismissed.

As a result, Linda and Rob became the target of much gossip and ill will. Morale and productivity in Rob's group plummeted, and absenteeism rose dramatically. The person Rob hired to replace Becky met with such a cool reception from the other team members that she resigned after only three weeks. Finally Linda decided something must be done. After discussing it with Rob, Linda met with Mark to tell him why his sister was dismissed and to ask his permission to share it in confidence with the rest of the department. Having suspected the reason for Becky's departure, Mark quickly consented.

In a group meeting, Linda led a three-part discussion to:

1. Announce the reason for Becky's dismissal.

2. Assign a committee to develop a plan to prevent similar problems in the future.

3. Announce a "MacMasters Night" at the ballpark, complete with tailgate party.

Within three weeks, the service department was back up to speed. Members of the "Houdini Team" (as their peers affectionately named them) devised a logical, nonthreatening theft-prevention procedure ... Becky's first replacement was recontacted and rehired (with explanations and apologies) ... Mark dealt personally with Becky's past customers to assure them that the expertise level they had come to expect had not dropped.

MacMasters Inc. had returned to normal.

CASE STUDY

C A S E   S T U D Y   A N A L Y S I S

CASE STUDY ANALYSIS

1. What would you have done in this situation?

2. How could you have avoided the morale problems you just read about?

3. Which of the six signals of lost momentum did service-department members communicate?

4. How did Linda respond?

Chances are Linda left this unfortunate encounter a much wiser leader. It's never a good idea to withhold information critical to team action and interaction. In this instance, everything worked out all right. But only a great meeting and a great recovery plan saved the service department.

A CHECKLIST FOR RESPONDING TO TEAM TROUBLES

Before you act on any apparent problem, especially when things seem to be out of control, always outline a plan. Great coaches don't react to situations. They give themselves time to think a problem through. Others might respond on impulse with their first thoughts, but a good coach plots exactly what course is needed to remedy the situation.

To help you keep a cool head in a crisis, answer these eight questions before you make a move:

1. What are the facts of the problem?

Be thorough with this one. Do your homework. The act of listing the facts can be the shortest route to revealing an obvious problem.

A form like the "Fact Recap Sheet" shown here provides a simple but solid way to organize your thoughts and shape a plan of action.

Fact Recap Sheet

Known problems	Numbered by importance	First step to take	Second step	What created the problem?	What would prevent recurrence?

2. What behaviors are at issue?

As you learned in Chapter 5, always focus on behavior, not attitudes. Identify the specific action (or inaction) causing the problems. Remember, even if Bill did the task grudgingly, he still did the task. If Bill made a mistake and accidentally didn't do the task, he didn't do the task. Certainly, the employee's attitude counts. Anyone would rather coach the team member who wanted to do well but failed. But when it comes to immediate problem-solving, it's the outcome, not the intent, you must focus on.

3. What are the consequences if things go unchanged?

Sometimes it's smarter to ignore a situation and see if it works itself out. Sounds irresponsible? Not really. You don't have to "rescue" everyone and resolve every situation. Occasionally a negative situation can be its own consequences ... its own deterrent to the problem happening again. Or maybe the problem is so small that consequences could cause *more* problems by drawing attention to it. Great coaches keep a finger on the team pulse ... without keeping the team under their thumbs.

4. Does the problem affect immediate objectives?

What jobs are in progress, and could this problem hurt them? If the answer is yes ... the problem *does* jeopardize immediate objectives ... you must mobilize all your energies to pinpoint the problem's source and a solution for it. If the problem doesn't jeopardize a project in progress, finish the tasks at hand before turning your attention to the disruption.

It's a little like the fire team putting aside 10 good hoses to fix one leaky hose while the warehouse burns down. Prioritize your response to the problem based on the threat to your most immediate goal.

5. How does the employee problem affect the long-range goal?

Asking yourself this question will help you put the behavior in question in perspective. The answer will provide a strong rationale when confronting and correcting the offender(s). How? By helping the employee see that her *behavior matters not because of how it matches your ideals as the leader but because of how it affects the organization's potential for success.* That's because the organization's mission or vision results in goals. Those goals and objectives reflect principles (such as, teamwork, integrity, respect for people, candid communications), and achieving the goals means behaving in a way that complements the principles.

Counterproductive behavior hurts — not just the *offender's* organizational standing but the organization itself — you, me, everybody. It's one thing for a team member to cost you a game — but that person must understand that her behavior can ultimately jeopardize the team's entire season!

For example, one person, believing she does not matter to the team, becomes complacent and begins showing up late for work. Everyone must cover for that team member.

6. What are the benefits of changed behavior?

What are the benefits of changed behavior to the project ... to the policies ... to the persons involved? You and your team members need to know what's in it for everyone if the problem goes away. That doesn't mean you must bribe a team member into compliance. It merely means showing the team member the logical conclusion of current vs. changed behavior.

For example, failure to stay alert on the job means a faulty part gets by ... which means a product will not perform properly ... which means customer's lives are complicated or endangered ... which means the company's reputation is tainted ... which means sales plummet ... which means people get laid off.

On the other hand, when faulty parts are caught and reworked, team quality rises ... consumer loyalty and trust increase ... sales climb ... people not only keep their jobs, but Christmas bonuses are given!

Surprisingly often, problem behavior is also ignorant behavior. When team members fully understand the ramifications of behavior, bad and good, the motivation to stick to company standards is much greater.

7. Am I in control and ready to discuss this situation?

Never, never, discuss a problem until you have control of your emotions. Damage for you, your team and your employee occurs when emotions prevail over logic and facts. If necessary, take a day ... or more ... to pull yourself together before acting on a problem. Yes, it's important to respond quickly to improper behavior, but not if you risk shattering a long-term solution by saying angry things you can't retract.

8. How can I support this employee?

This is not the first question that most coaches ask themselves when they prepare to respond to problem behavior. And although answering it may not produce an immediate change, it can promote long-term change. Why? Because meaningful support is almost always long-term — such as assigning a mentor to help the employee learn and improve, or giving additional training to help boost performance.

Supporting employees by helping them start positive behavior, not just stop negative activity, instills more company loyalty than any other single employee benefit — including salary!

"LOOK BEFORE YOU LEAP" CHECKLIST

Answer these questions before confronting an employee's
problem behavior. You'll be glad you did!

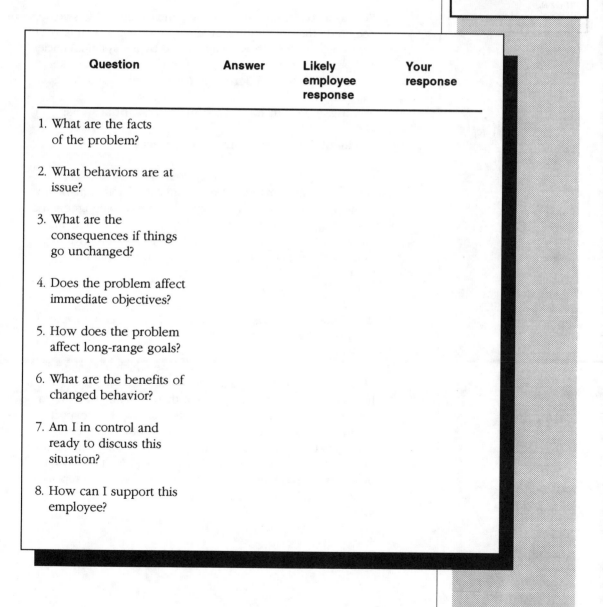

Question	Answer	Likely employee response	Your response
1. What are the facts of the problem?			
2. What behaviors are at issue?			
3. What are the consequences if things go unchanged?			
4. Does the problem affect immediate objectives?			
5. How does the problem affect long-range goals?			
6. What are the benefits of changed behavior?			
7. Am I in control and ready to discuss this situation?			
8. How can I support this employee?			

THE FREEING POWER OF TEAM PRIORITIES

Great coaches free their teams to do the right work. There is no greater freedom than putting tasks in proper priority. Unfortunately, in too many companies, management may feel in control but the employees don't at all. Employees aren't sure which tasks have top priority because everything is "hot."

You, as a coach, should create an atmosphere that lets your people do their work in an orderly, prioritized way. It is *your* job to protect them from being abused by the system. Policies and procedures often run on their own, and left unchecked, they can replace the human compassion every team needs.

Freeing your staff means taking five essential steps:

1. Identify and minimize "hot" projects.

If you've ever had someone give you a job marked "Urgent" and then another marked "Urgent" and still another marked "Urgent," you know what eventually happens. You ignore the word "Urgent." It's like the boy who cried wolf. People must know what the real priorities are or they won't do anything. You must make sure they understand exactly what the priorities are.

2. If the team deals with multiple bosses, coordinate priorities.

Don't force the team member to choose which boss she will please next. Come to an agreement with other managers about how priorities will be handled and then communicate this to your employee. If an urgent exception arises, don't expect your employee to handle it. Work it out with the other managers before handing the project over to the team member. Coming to such an agreement doesn't take long to do — not nearly as long as it takes to train a new employee to replace the one who has quit because she can't take the pressure any longer.

> **Great coaches free their teams to do the right work.**

3. Share the reason for changes — beat the "grapevine" to the punch.

The funny thing about the grapevine is how unfunny it can be. It encourages unfounded speculations like, "I bet this change is so they can cut jobs." The first thing you know, the "official" word is that the company is cutting jobs. Panic city! The moral: *You* control the information your people get. Be upfront and honest with them from the start. Ask whether they have any questions, and answer them. Put their minds at ease so they can focus on their work and not on the rumors.

4. Encourage team problem-solving.

The key to getting employees to work like a team is getting them to think like a team, with team goals ... team communication ... team recognition. The best way to start building this team thinking is to set goals that can be met only through teamwork. You might set goals for increasing group output or designing new procedures that will make everyone's job easier. As much as possible, let the team participate in the goal-setting process.

Ask everyone to take part in a brainstorming session. Ground rules should be: (1) Everyone is encouraged to contribute and (2) There's no such thing as a "bad" idea. Later, after all ideas have been listed, the group can select the idea most likely to succeed. This approach helps team members listen for each other's good ideas and gives everyone a chance to contribute to a team solution without fear of criticism.

A good team always can accomplish more than individual workers can on their own. And once employees discover the team synergy, group spirit and work efficiency that comes from working together, they'll want to keep the team spirit going.

> *There is no limit to how much good you can do if you don't care who gets the credit.*

5. Build in rewards for achievement.

When your schedule is so tight you can't eat lunch without feeling guilty, the day is not only less productive — it's just plain no fun. Team members experience the same sense of drudgery — and they are often less free to step off the treadmill (by delegating tasks, etc.) than you are. You must provide the light at the end of their tunnel. Otherwise, the potential for errors, low morale and employee burnout becomes great. How do you provide team relief from a priority-intensive schedule? Here are a few suggestions.

- **Take a team to lunch —**
  This event could mark the end of a successful project or just a fun and unexpected surprise.

- **Tickets please —**
  Buy season passes to a favorite event and offer them as ongoing awards for excellence.

- **Traveling trophy —**
  A funny poster, a small loving cup … anything can serve as a "team of the week" award. Will the current team or individual award-holder keep the trophy next week? Whose performance will win it next week? Watch your people have fun with these kinds of questions.

- **Family fun —**
  Plan a picnic where family and friends of team members can unwind and interact in a nonwork environment.

- **You name it —**
  Be creative! What would you like to look forward to if you were a member of your team? Chances are the team would like it, too — so go for it!

"Common sense is very uncommon."

— Horace Greeley

212

EXERCISE

In your workplace, what's the greatest hurdle in freeing team members to do "the right work right"? How can you use one of the techniques you've learned to help keep your staff focused on the job? Choose an area you want to improve and start planning for it today. For instance, you might want to circulate a memo whenever a change is announced, so everyone gets the information at the same time. Or you might want to develop a daily list of priorities for each person on your staff to put on her desk. Whatever you decide to work on, make it very specific ... very tangible.

Here are some simple but revealing questions to ask yourself that can help you anticipate problems, design preventive measures and put those measures into action:

1. **What areas currently fragment your team's work effort?**

2. **Based on the techniques you've just read, what's the most obvious way you could keep your staff focused and energized?**

3. **What specific steps will that take?**

4. **Which team members will be involved?**

5. **When will you start, and how will you measure your success?**

RIGHT THINKING ABOUT TEAM PURPOSE

In any leadership setting ... in any workforce ... two thinking styles can apply to the primary purpose of the team. One philosophy says the main goal of the team is to solve problems. The other approach says the purpose of teamwork is to improve team performance.

Which one lines up with the StaffCoaching™ Model? *Improving performance.* Why? Because if your main goal as a coach is to solve problems, you run the risk of becoming just a glorified fire extinguisher. You must go beyond solving problems to improving the performance that may be causing the problems. When you decide to *focus* on improving performance, you'll find yourself solving problems in the process. It's unavoidable.

To illustrate: Fine-tuning your fuel injection won't necessarily win the Indy 500. But deciding to win the Indy will *require* improved fuel injection. Another example: Teaching your team members conflict-resolution skills won't increase productivity. But giving them responsibility for increased productivity will demand conflict-resolution skills. Sure, you need both — but the order is all-important.

Get the idea? Make sure your team members do, too! Your goal and theirs should be to become a unified, objective-oriented, growing team. When that happens, your problems have met their match!

CHAPTER QUIZ

1. What are the four steps to developing a vision for your team?

2. List three signals of employee unrest.

3. Before you respond to a team problem or difficulty, what are eight preparatory steps you should consider?

4. What are five ways you can make it easier for your team to prioritize and follow through on tasks?

5. What one thing in this chapter will mean the most to your own team if you apply it this week?

216

CHAPTER 7

Stay in Control of Your StaffCoaching™ Role

"When performance improves, everyone wins. I succeed only when my team succeeds ... this clarifies my responsibility quite clearly on a day-to-day basis."   *— Kit Grant*

STAY IN CONTROL OF YOUR STAFFCOACHING™ ROLE

Even after you've coached, mentored and counseled as well as anyone could, people won't always do what they're supposed to do. That's not because the StaffCoaching™ Model is flawed — it's because people are flawed! We all are. But still, there's always a reason when team members fall short of standards.

Since 1976, Kit Grant has owned and managed his own business, in which he travels extensively and has found that the development of coaching skills has allowed him to maintain effective relations with his staff while not being with them on a consistent basis. Prior to starting his company, he worked in management positions in a food and beverage industry, in public education, and in a major communications organization. A dedicated learner who believes in life-long development and education, he knows the power of modeling, and through continuous self-improvement he has successfully instilled these values in those who work with him. He holds B.A., B.Ed., and M.Ed. degrees and is an active member of many professional associations dedicated to adult learning and expertise in speaking and training.

217

EXERCISE

With that in mind, let's try an exercise as we begin this chapter. Starting on this page are 11 reasons why even the best team members occasionally don't do what they're supposed to do. After each reason, you decide which of the StaffCoaching™ roles you would choose in order to respond best: coach, mentor or counselor.

Remember, the coaching role is to inspire and motivate team members who perform regularly above standard in one or more areas. The mentoring role is the instruction role — typically used for team members who perform about average. The counselor role is for confronting and correcting and is used for members who perform below standard in one or more areas.

Situations:

1. A team member doesn't know whether to do a certain task.

   _____

2. He doesn't know how to do it.

   _____

3. He thinks your way will not work.

   _____

4. He thinks his way is better.

   _____

5. He thinks something else is more important.

   _____

6. He sees no positive benefit for doing the task.

   _____

7. He thinks he is doing it right (but isn't).

   _____

8. He is rewarded for not doing it.

   _____

9. He is punished for doing it.

_____

10. No negative consequences exist for poor attempts.

_____

11. Obstacles exist that exceed his control.

_____

Role responses:

1. Mentor

2. Mentor

3. Mentor and counselor

4. Coach or counselor
   (maybe his way is better!)

5. Counselor

6. Coach (inspire and motivate)

7. Mentor and counselor
   (then coach)

8. Counselor and mentor
   Explanation:
   Some people complain so often, managers get tired of
   it and give the job to someone else. The moment you
   do that, you reward negative behavior.

9. Coach and counselor
   Explanation:
   These people never complain … they are always
   there. Consequently, they get the garbage jobs. Coach
   these people with gratitude, and perhaps let them vent
   their feelings to you as a counselor.

10. Counselor

11. Mentor, then coach

Whenever you face problems in dealing with your team members or whenever you want to achieve more through your people, you should look to the StaffCoaching™ Model for keys to the role that will best serve your purposes. Should you coach? Mentor? Counsel? Identify the level of performance and what role you should play, and you will be able to overcome many problems in leading your team to victory!

CHOOSING YOUR STAFFCOACHING™ ROLE BASED ON PERSONALITY

Pretend for a moment that you recently accepted responsibility for taking a successful product prototype to production in only three months. You've been assigned a production crew. As the StaffCoach™, it's your job to get the most out of each team member in the very short time you have to develop the product.

Using the StaffCoaching™ Model, you must decide what each member needs in terms of the roles you will play in his professional life. You'll respond to each of the following scenarios with one of five answers. Individuals will need to be either (1) coached, (2) mentored or (3) counseled. Plus we're going to add two more categories. You may need to (4) make some members coaches or (5) make some members mentors.

If you are responsible for more than 10 people, making team members coaches and/or mentors is a very important option for you. That's because having direct project responsibility for more than 10 people is very difficult. Adding coaches or mentors from the team ranks is like multiplying yourself. Multiplying (or delegating) is essential if you are going to be an effective StaffCoach™. To delegate successfully, you need to understand what to do before you delegate.

First, tell the team member what you expect. Make sure he understands your expectations.

Second, make the work valuable. Give the person a sense of value for being picked to do the job by ensuring the job is important.

> *"I've never been in a game where there wasn't enough glory for everybody."*
>
> *—Joe Paterno*

Finally, make the work doable. A great formula for making the work doable is the formula "V + E = M." It stands for Vision plus Enthusiasm equals Motivation.

First, share your own *vision* (direction) for the task at hand: the possible approaches to it … the various project phases … the hoped-for result. Make the vision open-ended, inviting the team member to add to or modify your ideas, encouraging his ownership of the project.

Next, *enthusiastically* communicate the benefits of the project as they relate specifically to the team member(s). As you personalize project benefits in this manner, you add "destination" to the direction you've provided. And when direction and destination are present, they always result in *motivation.*

If *motivation* is somehow absent from a project, you can generally find the reason for the problem by analyzing the vision (direction) and enthusiasm (destination) you have communicated or failed to communicate.

Notice that while you may make a team member a coach or mentor, you shouldn't make a team member a counselor. Why not? Because team members don't have the authority to confront or correct. That's your responsibility. So as you go through the next exercise, remember to answer in one of five ways:

1. **You respond to the team member as coach.**

2. **You respond as mentor.**

3. **You respond as counselor.**

4. **Team member serves as an assistant coach.**

5. **Team member serves as a mentor.**

> *"Partial commitment is dangerous."*
>
> — *Tom Osborne*

EXERCISE

Meet the production crew you coach — seven people with very special talents and needs! Based on what you learn from the remarks of each, decide how each person should be managed.

1. *"Hi, I'm Jeff Henry. I have 10 years of manufacturing experience and took part in developing the product prototype we're now putting into production."*

    I should use the following StaffCoaching™ role(s) in managing this person ...

    _____

    because ... _____
    _____

2. *"Hi. I'm Mike Smith. I'm really happy to have this job. I was recently hired specifically to work on this project."*

    I should use the following StaffCoaching™ role(s) in managing this person ...

    _____

    because ... _____
    _____

3. *"Hello, I'm Mary Smith. You just met my husband. I am a supervisor on this project. I've been told that I have excellent communication skills and a great work record."*

    I should use the following StaffCoaching™ role(s) in managing this person ...

    _____

    because ... _____
    _____

4. *"John Green here. All I want to say is that I'm going to be retiring soon."*

I should use the following StaffCoaching™ role(s) in managing this person ...

_____

because ... _____

_____

5. *"Hello. My name is Lee Chi. I don't speak English very good, but I work hard."*

I should use the following StaffCoaching™ role(s) in managing this person ...

_____

because ... _____

_____

6. *"My name is Jean Ehlers. I'm 21 years old and was hired about a year ago. I'm doing OK on my job, but I'm still very inexperienced as a machine operator."*

I should use the following StaffCoaching™ role(s) in managing this person ...

_____

because ... _____

_____

7. *"Jeri Sandberg here. I've been a design engineer with the company for five years. I can handle almost anything, except communicating with people ... and maybe getting to work on time."*

I should use the following StaffCoaching™ role(s) in managing this person ...

_____

because ... _____

_____

E
X
E
R
C
I
S
E

Answers:

1. Jeff needs coaching, right? He is certainly an above-standard team member. If you wrote that Jeff could also mentor someone, you're probably right. But to let him take on that responsibility will also require you to mentor him!

2. Mike may need your involvement in all three roles, but certainly as coach and mentor.

3. Mary is definitely a candidate for assistant coach. The skills are there. The work record is there. You will also want to coach and mentor her so she feels confident as an assistant coach. With that help, Mary could probably also mentor others, just as Jeff could.

4. Get the feeling that John's mind might be on other things? You need to coach and motivate him. If you do your job well, John's work experience will make him a great mentor.

5. Much of our culture is strange to Lee, but he's an outstanding worker. What does Lee need? He needs to be coached — inspired and motivated. "You're doing great, Lee. Keep it up." Lee will gradually need mentoring as well — maybe from Jeff or John.

6. Jean needs all the help you can give her — coaching, mentoring and counseling.

7. Jeri needs counseling, doesn't she? You'll have to confront her in the counseling role about her tardiness. Then someone ... maybe Mary (in light of her leadership and project-management skills) ... should mentor Jeri, especially in the area of communications. Once that's done, a good coach will look for ways to motivate her.

FOUR POINTS ON WHICH STAFFCOACHING™ STANDS OR FALLS

You need to remember four important points as you finish this book and put the StaffCoaching™ process to work. These are *the four "P's"* on which the entire StaffCoaching™ philosophy stands or falls — four steps in preparing for the inevitable resistance, objections and complaints you will regularly face.

The first P is for Plan.
You have to have a plan. Not to have a plan is to have a plan to fail!

The second P is for Practice.
You have to practice your plan. Practice and practice until it becomes a part of you.

The third P is Patience.
You must have patience. Patience will help you to act — not react.

The fourth P is Persistence.
Don't give up. Don't quit. Hang in there. Persistence will prevail!

The four "P's" are a great emergency outline for any action plan ... a great guideline for any managerial dilemma ... a great worksheet for thinking through a goal or objective. The four "P's" are powerful ... plain and simple. To illustrate, let's use the four "P's" as the StaffCoach's™ formula for dealing with team-member complaints.

1. You should *plan* for the inevitable. Complaints shouldn't come as a surprise to you as a successful coach. You should expect resistance, objections and gripes and be ready for them. Every assignment, project or procedure has the potential to generate such opposition. If you haven't planned for opposition by imagining what it might be ... and what your responses will be ... you'd better start.

> *True wisdom is like a river: the deeper it is, the less noise it makes.*

2. Once you know what you're going to say in response to resistance, you should *practice* those responses. Write down your responses ... say them out loud (in front of a mirror, if you like) ... but practice so you'll be entirely comfortable with your thinking and delivery.

3. After you know what you're going to say and have practiced it, then prepare to have *patience* when people finally do exhibit resistance in any form. (HINT: Your preparation up to this point will make having patience a lot easier!)

4. And, finally, you should use *persistence* in getting your point across. Don't imagine that every complainer will instantly buy in to your rationale just because you're the boss. If you believe your rationale, you'll stick to it — and then your team will believe it, too.

FIVE WAYS TO QUIET COMPLAINTS

Dealing with resistance isn't as ominous as it may sound — particularly if the resistance involves tasks. People generally need to hear five things from you to eventually quiet their complaints:

1. *Tell them why the job is important.* You read earlier (Chapter 5) about the need for job meaning. Once team members understand the importance of their jobs and how they contribute to the overall picture, their attitudes often change dramatically. To help make sure you avoid complaints by adequately communicating job importance, complete these three statements before addressing your team:

    a. This job will benefit the organization because

    _____ .

    b. This project will benefit every team member because

    _____ .

    c. Failing to do this job well (or at all) will result in these long-term negative circumstances:

    _____ .

2. *Tell them what the desired results are.* When people don't know your specific expectations, they don't know where they're going, when the job will end and whether or not they've done a good job. Being kept in the dark is very demoralizing. Always define desired results, and watch people respond positively. Here are five key facts your team will need to know to be motivated by the results you desire:

   - How will the results be achieved as a team? By individual team members?
   - Are the results one-time or ongoing? Explain.
   - How will the team know when the desired results are accomplished?
   - What team rewards are associated with the desired results?
   - What factors must be overcome to achieve the desired results (time constraints, equipment limitations, etc.)?

3. *Assign and define job authority.* If you give a team member responsibility for an aspect of a project, you must support him by also giving the authority to make it happen. Other team members must know this person has the authority. There are two basic ways to publicize who's in charge: by memo or by personal announcement to the members concerned. In either approach, you must answer the following three questions to everyone's satisfaction to make sure the authority you're about to transfer "sticks."

   a. How will the authority be used on a daily basis?
   b. Exactly how are team members expected to respond?
   c. What are the benefits of responding to this new authority — and what are the consequences of failing to respond?

If you want to develop a potential leader and maximize the chances of project success, let the person have the authority to do the job ... not just the responsibility.

Problems are those things people see when they take their eyes off the goal.

227

4. *Agree on deadlines.* Don't assume when you give an assignment that people will automatically know when it's due. Spell out deadlines clearly. Don't leave it to chance. Chance has never been a dependable employee!

To make sure deadlines are M.E.T., you should ...

Monitor milestones
Build in periodic progress checks before the project completion date.

Energize efforts
If project phases are lagging, suggest ideas and/or change procedures or personnel to bring the project back up to speed.

Team triumphs
Did you meet the deadline? Find some way to celebrate it. The celebration doesn't have to be a big deal — a quick meeting to acknowledge key players ... an inexpensive lunch at a favorite out-of-the-office gathering place, whatever. The important thing is this: Don't let a deadline victory slip by without a "team triumph" celebration.

5. *Provide feedback.* Ask your staff to give you feedback ... written or spoken ... on how the job is going. How could it have been planned better? How do team members feel you have responded to their needs? The act of seeking ideas and opinions through open-ended questions will boost the morale of your team more than the greatest pep talk ever written!

APPLYING THE FOUR "P'S"

If the four "P's" work at all, they must work for you. So let's put them to the test. This exercise is designed to prepare you for your next major StaffCoaching™ challenge. You probably already know what that challenge is — or at least what it's likely to be.

The road to success is marked with tempting parking places.

In the box below, list the top three job situations you wish would never happen but feel certain will happen … and maybe soon. That might mean announcing a project everyone hates. Maybe it means dealing decisively with ongoing, inappropriate behavior from an individual or the group. Now pick the situation you feel least able to control and fill in an approach to each of the four "P's" listed below. Ask yourself:

a. _____

b. _____

c. _____

1. **What PLAN can I think of that might make the situation as painless as possible? (It's always good to have an alternate plan, too.)**

   _____

   _____

2. **What specific PRACTICE would best prepare me for the upcoming encounter or occurrence (working through a speech? arming myself with research or data? etc.)?**

   _____

   _____

3. **How is my PATIENCE likely to be tested? How can I be ready for the impatience I will undoubtedly feel? How will I counter it?**

   _____

   _____

4. **How will I demonstrate PERSISTENCE in presenting my plan or position? What responses to hypothetical resistance or complaints can I arm myself with?**

   _____

   _____

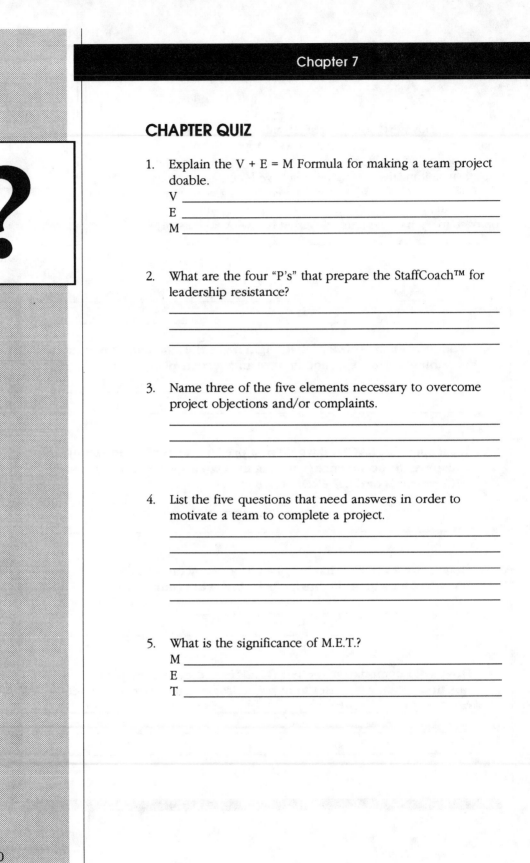

CHAPTER QUIZ

1. Explain the V + E = M Formula for making a team project doable.

    V _____

    E _____

    M _____

2. What are the four "P's" that prepare the StaffCoach™ for leadership resistance?

    _____

    _____

    _____

3. Name three of the five elements necessary to overcome project objections and/or complaints.

    _____

    _____

    _____

4. List the five questions that need answers in order to motivate a team to complete a project.

    _____

    _____

    _____

    _____

    _____

5. What is the significance of M.E.T.?

    M _____

    E _____

    T _____

CHAPTER 8

Conclusion

"The manager who is a coach must realize that his or her single greatest asset is his or her people."
— Joe Gilliam

StaffCoaching™ is a never-ending process. Once you achieve new levels of performance, those levels become the new standard. You start the process all over again.

And as you've probably already gathered, you don't have to perform your StaffCoaching™ roles in any certain order. You won't always begin as a coach with a person, then move to mentor or to counselor — or vice versa. You use the role you need at that moment to match the problem.

And through it all, remember it's your responsibility as the StaffCoach™ to exhibit a positive attitude. Coaches imprint values on the people who belong to their team. And values that are *real* values invariably translate into team activity that supports company objectives. How do you project these positive values? By:

> **Teamwork is a journey, not a destination.**

Joe Gilliam has been a management consultant and seminar leader for 14 years. Prior to becoming a consultant, he served in management and leadership positions in three organizations. Joe's unique style as a presenter models for the participants the qualities needed to be a coach. Joe has trained managers in coaching skills for McDonald's, Domino's Pizza, Georgia Power, Alabama Power, Northwest Airlines, The Army, and The Airforce.

(1) **Setting an example**
(2) **Being fair and equitable**
(3) **Seeking the participation and involvement of each team member**

As we conclude this book, let's take a look at three scenarios. Each one reflects one of the three ways of projecting a positive StaffCoach™ philosophy. Each scenario is done first the "right way" and then the "wrong way." See if you can spot the StaffCoach™ techniques that *aren't* implemented ... as well as those that *are* implemented in projecting a positive philosophy to team members.

"STAFFCOACH™ VALUES" SCENARIOS

1. Setting an example...

THE RIGHT WAY:

Coach:
Well, let's take a break and pick back up in about 10 minutes, OK?

(as all leave but Jim)
I think we're getting some good ideas for this new project, don't you?

Jim:
Yes. No thanks to Nancy.

Coach:
What do you mean?

Jim:
Nothing she's said has been new. They're the same ideas we heard and rejected last time we had a brainstorming session.

Coach:
Oh, I don't know. I think some of her thoughts have potential.

Jim:
Give me a break.

Coach:
Jim, just because an idea wasn't quite right for one project doesn't mean it couldn't work for another.

Jim:
If you say so.

Coach:
Relax and enjoy the session. Or better yet, try to think of something you could add to ideas you don't like that could make them better. You're good at things like that, just like Nancy is good at telephone sales.

Scenario analysis

What did the StaffCoach™ do right?

_____

_____

What would you have done differently? Why?

_____

_____

What should the StaffCoach™ follow-up be as a result of this scenario?

_____

_____

THE WRONG WAY:

Coach:
Well, let's take a break and pick back up in about 10 minutes, OK?

(as all leave but Jim)
I think we're getting some good ideas for this new project, don't you?

S
C
E
N
A
R
I
O

Jim:
Yes. No thanks to Nancy.

Coach:
Well, everybody has bad days once in a while.

Jim:
Bad? Nothing she's said has been new. They're the same ideas we heard and rejected last time we had a brainstorming session.

Coach:
We've got to be patient with her. Besides, we're making good progress in spite of her. Let's just let her talk once in a while and hope we keep getting good ideas from the rest of us.

Scenario analysis

What did the StaffCoach™ do wrong?

_____

_____

What would you have done differently? Why?

_____

_____

What should the StaffCoach™ follow-up be as a result of this scenario?

_____

_____

2. Being fair and equitable ...

THE RIGHT WAY:

Jean:
Cliff, Rita just told me someone would probably have to
visit the Dallas client next weekend. Is that true?

Cliff:
Yes. I just heard about it an hour ago myself.

Jean:
Well, I know it's my turn to go, but my brother and his
family are going to be in town that weekend. Can you
please get someone else to do it?

Cliff:
I can ask if someone would like to trade with you and ...

Jean:
No one will! Everybody hates that client.

Cliff:
Well, I don't think we can really say that, just because ...

Jean:
Why don't you send the new guy? He hasn't been
assigned a spot on the travel roster yet. He'd probably
consider it an honor.

Cliff:
No, I don't think that would be good. I want him to travel
with someone else a few times until he learns the ropes.
But I'll tell you what I will do.

Jean:
What?

Cliff:
If nobody will trade with you, I think I could probably go
to Dallas that weekend.

Scenario analysis

What did Cliff do right?

_____

_____

What would you have done differently? Why?

_____

_____

_____

What should the StaffCoach™ follow-up be as a result of this scenario?

_____

_____

THE WRONG WAY:

Jean:
Cliff, Rita just told me someone would probably have to visit the Dallas client next weekend. Is that true?

Cliff:
Yes. I just heard about it an hour ago myself.

Jean:
Well, I know it's my turn to go, but my brother and his family are going to be in town that weekend. Can you please get someone else to do it?

Cliff:
I can ask if someone would like to trade with you and ...

Jean:
No one will! Everybody hates that client. Why don't you send the new guy? He hasn't been assigned a spot on the travel roster yet.

Cliff:

I don't know. That could be a little like throwing a sheep to the wolves.

Jean:

Or it could be the best thing that's ever happened. He's a Mexican American and the client is, too. It might end up being the perfect match.

Cliff:

Umm. Well, OK. But this is just between you and me — and if we lose a promising new guy because of this, it will be your job to find a new one.

Scenario analysis

What did Cliff do wrong?

_____

_____

What would you have done differently? Why?

_____

_____

What should the StaffCoach™ follow-up be as a result of this scenario?

_____

_____

C. Seeking participation and involvement

THE RIGHT WAY:

Bob:
So how much computer equipment is missing?

John:
About $6,000 worth. Two units and a hard disk.

Bob:
Any ideas about how it happened?

John:
None. Except I know it wasn't anyone on the team. Ever since you gave us the key to the equipment room, each of us has taken turns with hourly inventory.

Bob:
What does security say about it?

John:
That it was probably an inside job. But I still say that it wasn't one of the team members, Bob. No one would betray the trust the company gave us by giving us access to that room.

Bob:
I believe that, too. I certainly have no reason to think otherwise.

John:
But you probably want the key back, right?

Bob:
No. I want your team to work out a system with security that makes it impossible for someone to get out of here with $6,000 worth of equipment. And one more thing.

John:
What's that?

Bob:
Tell the team I really like the increase figures I saw last week.

Scenario analysis

What did Bob do right?

_____

_____

What would you have done differently? Why?

_____

_____

What should the StaffCoach™ follow-up be as a result of this scenario?

_____

_____

THE WRONG WAY:

Bob:
So how much computer equipment is missing?

John:
About $6,000 worth. Two units and a hard disk.

Bob:
Any ideas about how it happened?

John:
None. Except I know it wasn't anyone on the team. Ever since you gave us the key to the equipment room, each of us has taken turns with hourly inventory.

Bob:
Well, I'm afraid I'm going to need that key back … at least until we can prove it was no one on the team.

S
C
E
N
A
R
I
O

John:
I wish you wouldn't, Bob. It will look like you suspect everyone.

Bob:
Maybe. But I can't risk another theft while we're investigating the first one. Upper management would think I was crazy!

Scenario analysis

What did Bob do wrong?

_____

_____

What would you have done differently? Why?

_____

_____

What should the StaffCoach™ follow-up be as a result of this scenario?

_____

_____

BIRDS OF A FEATHER WORK TOGETHER

Have you ever studied geese? Have you ever watched geese fly in a "V" formation? Ornithologists have uncovered some very interesting facts about why geese fly in that "V." First of all, as each bird flaps its wings, it creates an uplift for the bird immediately following it. By flying together in a "V" formation, each goose adds at least 71 percent more distance or range to its flight ability. Isn't that incredible? They go 71 percent farther if they go together.

Do you see the parallel to operating as a team? Teams must stick together. If we don't, we're in trouble. We want to go as far as we can ... to get the best results. And we can only do it as a team.

Science has revealed something else about these large feathered friends. Whenever a goose deviates from the formation, it gradually feels the drag of trying to go it alone. As soon as it returns to formation, it again takes advantage of the "lift" power provided by the wings of the other birds. And, finally, when the lead goose in these formations grows tired, it rotates to the rear of the formation, and another goose takes up the point temporarily.

Are you encouraging stragglers to take advantage of ... even re-enter ... your team formation? Are your strongest fliers providing needed lift? Are you helping develop leadership skills by "rotating to the rear" occasionally so others can get a feel for "flying point"?

Geese can teach us a lot about teamwork.

The StaffCoaching™ Model helps you know when to impart certain values. If someone is turning in a performance that is above standard, you communicate specific values through the role of a coach. If it's standard performance, use the role of mentor. If it's substandard, you become a counselor. To be effective, you have to be flexible ... sensitive to the needs of your people and able to meet them at their level.

To be a great StaffCoach™, you have to understand the ways to motivate your staff from the sidelines ... to cheer your players on to their highest levels of achievement ... and to love every minute of it!

Then watch your team start winning!

*I*NDEX

A
ABC, 51
authority-driven thinkers, 134

B
Beecher, Henry Ward, 45
behavior modification
    Five Steps to, 183-185
    "Look Before You Leap" Checklist, 209
    worksheet, 186
Birds of a Feather Work Together, 241

C
Carlyle, Thomas, 45
Cather, Willa, 142
Churchill, Winston, 42
clarity, 2-3, 9, 17, 84
Coaching Role, 71-73
    Eight Hurdles to Performing Your Role, 102-113
    Role in Affirming Team, 94-96
    Role in Clarifying Expectations, 81-94
    Role in Communicating Involvement and Establishing
    Trust, 74-81

Role in Motivating and Inspiring Team, 98-102
What to Expect When You're Doing It Right, 116-120
communication
    "3-1-3" Method, 87-88
    10 freeing questions, 79-80
    asking questions, 89
    Clarifying Expectations and Verifying Understanding, 82-84
    improvement, 100
    methods, 85-86
complaints
    Five Ways to Quiet, 226
confidence-building, 2, 8, 17
confidentiality, 2, 15, 18, 75
confrontation, 161-164
    Five-Step Process, 164-168
    "Look Before You Leap" Checklist, 209
    Philosophy of, 161,
    Problem-Solving Discussion Aid, 166
counseling
    10 Freeing Essentials of Face-to-Face, 176-179
    Benefits of Counseling worksheet, 191
    Four Keys to Effective, 157-159
    Evaluation Exercise, 175
    How to Ask Questions, 187
    Recognizing the Results, 189

D

deductive thinkers, 135
Devine, Dan, 71
Disraeli, Benjamin, 190
Dryden, John, 108
Dugger, Jim, 60

E

emotional thinkers, 137-139
employees
    aptitude, 130
    keeping team goals in front of, 105-106
    Knowing Character and Capabilities, 36-44
    valuing the, 57
Epictetus, 2

F

"15-5-10" Formula, 131, 149
feedback
    effective, 61
    listening to, 92
    providing, 228
    Opportunity for, worksheet, 62
Five Golden Questions of Leading People, 57
Fournies, Ferdinand, 50

G

goals
    consistent with organizational direction, 104
    keeping in front of employees, 105-106
    lack of, 103-104, 114
    memo, 9
    mutuality, 8
    shared, 99
    team goals exercise, 106
Greeley, Horace, 212

H

Hazlitt, William, 226
Hubbard, Kin, 77

I

Interview Recap Form, 39
intuitive thinkers, 139
involvement, 2, 14, 18
Irving, Washington, 214

J

Job Phase Progress Report, 148
Joubert, 92

K

Kelly, George, 10
knee-jerk response
    how to monitor, 118-119
    obedience in employees, 134

L

leadership
  detached, 103, 114
  Five Golden Questions of Leading People, 57
  patient, 129
Lincoln, Abraham, 96
listening, 92-93
  Five Principles of, 58-59
  Jim Dugger book, 60
Lombardi, Vince, 38

M

Mackovic, John, 72
MBWA, 74,109
mentoring, 127-151
  3 key phases of, 141-142
  "10-60-90" Principle, 141-149
  "15-5-10" Formula, 131
  Effective Mentoring Worksheet, 154
  mentoree task worksheet, 145
  Outcome of Effective, 149
  Treasure of, 155
M.E.T., 228
Moomaw, Don, 13
mutuality, 2, 8-9, 17

O

On-the-job Evaluation Form, 41
Osborne, Tom, 221
outcome-contrast, 85

P

Paterno, Joe, 220
patience, 2, 13, 18, 113, 225
Performance Assessment worksheet, 34
perspective, 2, 10, 18
Peters, Tom, 74
"pro-active" mindset, 60, 151
Project Recap and worksheet, 111-112

Q

questions
   asking, 89-90, 187
   Five Golden Questions of Leading People, 57
   open-ended, 169-170, 187-188
Quizzes, Chapter, 31, 70, 125, 156, 192, 215, 230

R

RAP, 27
Reports on Progress worksheet, 92
respect, 2, 15, 18
rewards, 77, 132, 173-174, 185, 212
risk, 2, 11, 18
role-playing, 85

S

scientific thinkers, 140
sensory thinkers, 136
StaffCoaching™
   10 key attributes of successful, 55-56
   10 Values of Successful, 2
   Choosing Your Role Based on Personality, 220-221
   Five insights of High Performance, 23
   four "P's," 225-226, 228-229
   Manager's Role as, 1
   Six Pitfalls to Your Success, 48-53
   staying in control of role, 217-219
   Style Inventory, 46-47
   trouble-shooting, 198, 205, 225-226
   Values Scenarios, 232-240
StaffCoaching Model™ , 33-35, 55, 157, 195
Supervisory Observation Form, 43
supportiveness, 2, 5, 17
Swift, Jonathan, 196
synergy, 26

T

"3-1-3" Method, 87-88
"10-60-90" Principle, 141, 149
Talent Inventory, 26
team
    Booster forms, 97
    coach's role in affirming, 94-96
    Freeing Power of Priorities, 210-212
    goals, 103
    instilling vision, 195, 197
    Member Questionnaire, 44
    recognizing trouble, 198-201
    responding to trouble, checklist, 205-208
    Right Thinking About Purpose, 214
team-building
    10 Tools for Building a Solid Foundation, 55-65
    verifying understanding, 89-91
thinking, methods of
    authority-driven, 134
    deductive, 135
    emotional, 137
    intuitive, 139
    scientific, 140
    sensory, 136
    thinker type analysis, 140

V

V + E = M, 220
values, 1
    of Successful StaffCoach™ , 2
    StaffCoach™ values worksheet, 22
    Tracing Your Personal Values History, worksheet, 20
    What You Value Will Impact Your Team, 19
Valvano, Jim, 168

W

"Walking Alongside," 127, 133
Walsh, Bill, 4
Whipple, Edwin, 65
W.I.N., 104
Wooden, John, 129